LIFE AFTER DIVORCE

FINDING LIGHT IN LIFE'S DARKEST SEASON

LEAH SILVERII

SCOTT SILVERII

Five Stones University

COPYRIGHT

This book is dedicated to Matt Sessoms. Your heart, passion, and wisdom has changed lives. It changed ours. Thank you.

That is why a man leaves his father and mother and is united to his wife, and they become one flesh.

Genesis 2:24 (NIV)

CONTENTS

INTRODUCTION

Think marriage is hard?

Try a second marriage. Now add children from different families, opposing careers, two homes, finances, exes, and child support. Did we forget to mention in-laws?

Surviving divorce, reclaiming your worth, and rebuilding life with another person is as challenging as it is a wonderful opportunity to see God's will at work. Leah and I know what it feels like to hit the dark and bumpy patches of life, but we thank Him for being a redeeming God of second chances.

Divorce is a difficult topic, and it's possible you're still going through the process or struggling with the aftermath. We felt led to reach out in these times because we've not only been there, but we both wish there'd been someone or something like this book to offer us straight truths in turbulent times.

We're not going to sugarcoat it, or encourage you to say sweet things about yourself in a mirror. Is divorce and remarriage God's plan for family? Of course not. A healthy, nuclear family is what He wants for us. But there have been many families in the bible that didn't meet

God's plan, but He extended grace and blessed them because they sought His heart. And better yet, God used these "less than ideal" families like theirs and ours to build His kingdom.

We want to encourage you that through God's love and your faithfulness, it is possible to find healing, hope, and happiness post-divorce. Our F-A-I-T-H model for recovery to romance provides practical steps and biblical truths for the season of transitioning from defeat to victory.

Although you may feel like it, you're not alone. The next time you're in church, look around and you'll see many believers who have been divorced or who are remarried with blended families. While most churches have a heart for the hurting, few provide the direct support to the divorced, or those remarrying and blending families. The effects of those divorces extend beyond single parents, as studies show thirty-five percent of children from divorced parents leave the church all together.

We're not theologians. We're people just like you, who love God, but who make mistakes. We've endured the tragedy of divorce and know without fail that Christ has blessed us with each other. We recognize the opportunity to glorify Him by celebrating our marriage and blended family. Now, we want to help and encourage others by sharing our journey.

There is always hope,

Scott and Leah Silverii

1

THE REALITY OF DIVORCE

"So do not fear, for I am with you: do not be dismayed, for I am your God. I will strengthen you and help you; I will uphold you with my righteous right hand."
Isaiah 41:10

I couldn't believe it. I'd grown up with this girl and her family. They were good people. How could something so horrible happen?

It was simple. *Divorce.*

Rather than my friend subjecting her little boy and girl to the pain of divorce, and the possibility of a new woman assuming a part-time role as their stepmother, she decided to end the lives of her young children.

While heartbreaking, this wasn't the only incident I'd experienced because of divorce in my over twenty-five years of policing. The majority of extremely brutal murders and physical attacks were results of domestic violence. These assaults usually stemmed from unstable marriages that involved divorce, unless death or jail came first.

Friends, we're not talking about schoolyard crushes that fade before the cafeteria bell rings. Divorce is the devil's prize. He delighted at deception in the Garden of Eden, and continues to chalk up victory after soul-crushing victory.

If you haven't figured it out already, divorce hurts more than our children, pride, or bank accounts. It hurts our very spirit because of a broken covenant with God.

At least with a death there is closure to help ease the loss. Comparing divorce to death is an appropriate analogy because the loss felt through divorce is a powerfully emotional and life-changing event. And unfortunately, it's a fairly common occurrence.

Statistics show that more than fifty percent of the married population find themselves divorced after a first marriage. Sixty-seven percent of second marriages and seventy-three percent of third marriages end in divorce as well. Although the failure rate remains high and marriage is under attack as an outdated institution, a loving relationship is still what people desire most.

People were created to enter into eternal relationships that mirror the way God relates to us. According to *MarriageToday's* Pastor Jimmy Evans, our four deepest needs can be fulfilled in a bible-based marriage: Acceptance, Identity, Security and Purpose. When this four-legged table begins missing one or more of these needs, the spouses begin looking elsewhere.

The numbers prove people still believe in retrying their luck at the institution of marriage, but I fear the actual wedding celebration has become the finish line instead of the starter's pistol. To make sure you don't or won't get stuck at the starting line, we will guide you from your post-divorce recovery to a point of a Christ-centered opportunity for new romance if that is the desire of your heart.

I still recoil at the youthful arrogance wrapped around preparations for my first wedding. The running joke was that we'd host a Southern Baptist wedding and a Catholic reception for the alcohol and partying. I'd rarely seen the inside of a church leading up to our ceremony, so to associate anything with faith was ignorance. But as college sweethearts, marrying was the next logical step after graduation, right?

The truth was, neither of us were ready to marry. We knew nothing of Christ, covenants, or serving Him as the head of the relationship. After the first pastor we'd asked refused to marry us, we eventually found one who agreed to perform the ceremony, and the party planning began. It was set to be the biggest booze bash since my last college fraternity brouhaha. Who cared that we had no home, careers, or pre-marital counseling—we were gettin' hitched.

The funny, yet fair, thing about statistics is that they don't care who you are. We divorced after about eight years. My comment at the time of the divorce was something stupid about having beaten the national seven-year average. I should've been more concerned about my wife and our four-year-old son.

In the United States, not even age and assumed wisdom prevents divorce. Men and women, aged 50 to 69, remarry at a rate twenty percent higher than other age group demographics. Guess what? They still divorce at the same rate as others for second marriages. The U.S. seems to engage in a pattern of marriage, divorce, and remarriage, or something I like to call the marriage-go-round.

If you've bought this book, we can assume that you're divorced. It's an important distinction to make because if you are still married, we want to encourage you to do everything in God's will to save your marriage. We know there are reasons for divorce such as abandonment, abuse and adultery. But even in these circumstances there can be restoration through Christ.

If you are divorced, we will assume you may also be somewhere along the continuum from recovering to dating again to even a new marriage. We'll take you through the processes so you'll be best equipped to not make the same mistakes in your next marriage.

There is also help on how to successfully blend your families and give your children a happy, whole, and healthy marriage they can look to as an example. Yes, you can be an example the second time around!

We also assume you already know what divorce does to children—they tend to suffer academically and have more behavioral problems, they're prone to be arrested, and more likely to live in poverty as an adult. It can also affect their future relationships. The statistics aren't in their favor.

But there's good news! Number one: God overcomes all. Number two: adults who enter into a healthy, Christ-centered marriage, who pray together and put God first, marriage second, and children third, may stem or reverse the negative legacy of their children.

Experience shows that the loving, bible-based marriage example shown to children is vital for their own future relationships. The cycle of failure and loss can be mitigated by positive examples with loving parents, even blended, where the husband and wife lead by the example of strength through marital unity.

The Pain of Loss

I feel like we should repeat this every few pages or so, but time does not heal all wounds. Unresolved pain only manifests itself into deeper and more debilitating injuries. Let's talk about getting through the pain and bringing the healing light of Christ to what is hurting you.

Satan knows just what buttons to push. After my first wife and I split, the old serpent slithered in, and taunted me with fear of loneliness and failure. He knew my pain remained great and rumbled just below the surface over the loss of my family. The devil played my pride so I would stay chained to the bowels of hell, and ruin any chance of reconciliation with her.

I needed acceptance. What was a thirty-one-year-old man going to do as a single father, that anyone would ever desire him? I was damaged goods, but worse, I was damned to live the rest of my life alone. There was no one to guide me back into God's arms. But there was the wicked, ancient one willing to lead me into the arms of another type of affirmation. Sexual sin and fabricated fulfillment laid a faulty foundation for my rebound, second marriage.

With still fresh ink on my divorce decree, I hustled to the pastor's office to get married. My parents, family and friends begged me not to do it. The more roadblocks those who cared about me put up, the more determined I was to smash through them. My last words before walking out of my office to meet the pastor and my soon-to-be second ex-wife was, "What the hell."

And it was. For the next month and a half, the farce of marriage was a living hell. The pain satan chased me around with during my divorce was nothing compared to the blow torch he ignited in the second failed marriage.

This would be my second divorce in less than a year. Now I really was damaged goods, and the consequences of an unholy matrimony included even more long-term consequences. I knew it had to end. Still, I was so afraid to walk into an empty house...again. It felt like I was dying, and maybe I had—inside.

Swiss-American psychiatrist, Elisabeth Kübler-Ross's 1969 book, *On Death and Dying,* serves as the gold standard for understanding grief through loss. It will also serve as a litmus test for dealing with divorce.

The truth is, everyone handles divorce in their own way. One thing is certain, if there was even the most minimal emotional investment between a couple, the same stages of coping with loss are going to show themselves in varying degrees of impact.

The stages of grief are a loose framework to gauge the movement into and out of the cycle. Some cycles begin at the first mention of divorce and continue at a consistent pace until you've gained freedom from your past. Others may be delayed by months or years. We can't stress enough that this isn't a competition to see who gets over it the fastest. Recovery is based solely on the individual, not the theory.

Leah and I want to walk you through the stages toward recovery from divorce. Each stage illustrates the role God plays in your restoration, but equally as important is the light He shines in your times of greatest darkness.

> *"Yea, though I walk through the valley of the shadow of death, I will fear no evil: for thou art with me; thy rod and thy staff they comfort me."*
> *Psalm 23:4*

As David wrote in this Psalm, you will indeed walk through the valley while moving along the process of divorce. I stumbled through the dark valley of divorce and made the mistake of thinking it couldn't get any worse. I was so wrong so often you'd think I'd stop saying it.

You'd be wrong.

It might be an inherent optimism, but people in crisis often fail to understand the severity of their situation. Conversely, others overreact, and that's just as bad, but in general, you only know what you know. So unless you're an old pro at divorces, you've probably become mired in an unrealistic assessment of your situation.

People in crisis often mistakenly blame God for their circumstance and question why He hadn't swooped in to rescue them. God will not force Himself into your life. It's the whole free will thing. We want it, He gives it, and now we use it to our detriment more than we should. Putting off your relationship with Christ will only intensify and prolong your suffering. He is patiently waiting for you.

> *"'Behold, I stand at the door and knock; if anyone hears My voice and opens the door, I will come in to him and will dine with him, and he with Me."*
> *Revelation 3:20*

The merciful beauty of this is that once you welcome Jesus back into your life, He doesn't linger outside kicking a toe against the threshold debating whether or not He loves you anymore. He does love you, and will rush in to comfort you through this season in your life.

I shared earlier the fear of losing at marriage again, so I avoided home until my second wife vacated the place. That night, very late at night, I was so afraid to walk into an empty house I became overcome with dread and guilt. You have to understand this dynamic to fully appreciate the dilemma.

I was a two hundred and fifty pound, powerlifting martial artist who was working as an undercover agent and SWAT cop. I was living the ultimate alpha male lifestyle of adrenaline-laced danger and risk, so failure was not an option. Except that it was, and I had zero control over it. Shame of failure was so deeply embedded at the thought of embarrassing my parents, family, co-workers and myself, that I started thinking through the process of suicide.

I remember sitting in my undercover police vehicle at the darkened far end of a shopping center parking lot. I'd worked an entire shift and then overtime to keep my mind occupied. I knew my second ex-wife was cleaning out the house I'd shared with my first wife.

We'd lasted a whopping one and a half months. I would've been surprised to have paint left on the walls when I got home. It was a completely toxic relationship and it had to end.

Blares from the police radio in the background refocused my thoughts to the reality of what awaited me. I had been divorced before, and I knew all too well how damaging it was. I was still locked into that painful cycle of loss. The rebound relationship didn't carry pain for it's failure, but it acted as a catalyst to reignite the wounds from my first marriage's failure.

Can you see how complex human emotion and actions outside of God's will can get? I'd fallen too far and there was no longer an option of turning back. I'd caused too much damage to repair, and worse than knowing it was my fault, was having no idea how to change to fix it. To fix me. There was only one thing left to do. I wasn't afraid to die, but I did fear leaving my young son. That old devil also has the skills to deceive you into rationalizing sin and self-destruction.

Satan taunted, "He'll be better off without you."

I turned off the police radio, and closed my eyes. Hot tears welled up in the corners of my eyes and began to fall into my lap. This was the end to an endless misery.

But then, God whispered, "Come home."

Never will I forget God calling me to come home. Personally, I was shocked to hear His voice. I'd been away from Him for a long time because of the unconfessed sin in my life. But in that moment, I was desperate and fractured, and I cried out to Him. I was so ashamed of the mess I'd made of my life.

I creeped back down my street, and pulled beneath a pitch black carport. Her car was gone. There was relief, but my gut wrenched into a twisted knot. My hand trembled while unlocking the front deadbolt. The lights were off, and I sensed a spirit inside. I was keenly aware of what satan's oppression had held over me, but this wasn't the familiar stench of fear.

I crashed to my knees just inside the doorway. There was no furniture, paintings or sound. Just darkness. I'd avoided God for years. They had been turbulent, violent, shameful years, but I cried out in the name of Jesus. I confessed through tears and coughing sobs of guilt over the pitifully, harmful life I'd been living. In that moment of desperation, I heard His voice.

"Be still."

Despite my mistakes, God's plan for me didn't expire in 1998 at the far end of a shopping center parking lot. No, He knew I needed to stick around, so Leah and I could write this to you somewhere in the future.

Our prayer is for you to avoid the mistakes we, and millions of others make, by desperately or stubbornly choosing to walk through this valley alone. Christ is waiting to guide you by the hand. Just reach out to Him. So, with one hand holding onto Christ and the other flipping the pages of this book, let's head forward, shall we?

One more thing. Before we head on to the next chapter, I felt it so important for Leah to directly lend her voice to this topic, that I asked her to share with you. This, and some other chapters will end with what we call, Leah's Story.

While we collaborated as equal partners, my experiences naturally flavored the content with my telling. Her heart and wisdom will speak to you like only she can. Her vision is a blessing to me, as I know it will be to you.

Leah's Story

When Scott asked me to give my testimony at the end of these chapters, I wasn't entirely sure what to say, or how to go about saying it. But the truth is, I've been through a divorce, and though the divorce process wasn't the lowest point in my life or most traumatic, it runs a close second. It changed the person I am forever.

Hindsight is an amazing thing. When I look back on my first marriage and subsequent divorce, I realize that the divorce wasn't out of the blue. I can pinpoint exactly when the process started. It was 2007, and I remember after a terrible fight saying the words, "At this point, we're only married because of the kids."

That was the first time I thought about suicide. It was also the first time I wondered whether or not my children would be okay without me. We stayed together another six years, going on with our separate lives. For the kids.

During those six years, I straightened my spine, buried my anger, and focused on work and the kids. Does that sound familiar? I'd put all areas of my life into little boxes—work, children, travel, then rinse and repeat. Somewhere in there was a husband who was doing his own thing too.

And then my father died.

All of a sudden, it wasn't so easy to compartmentalize anymore. For those last years of my marriage, I'd put my emotions on hold and just powered through. I'd told myself I was tough. That I didn't need anyone. That I was independent. That I could handle everything myself. I told myself I could do all of that and write six books a year, travel all over the world for book signings, and raise four children. Piece of cake.

Eventually, I ran out of compartments. I remember telling a friend during that time that I felt like I was drowning, and no matter how much I tried to come up for air I couldn't do it. I said that statement over and over to people in my family, but the words fell on deaf ears. One of the counselors I went to during that time said that those words should've been a warning sign to the people who loved me. In reality, it told me more about the character of the people who loved me than anything else. Forgiveness is part of the healing process.

I was the consistent one in my family—the stable one—the one everyone counted on to get things done. I was the full-time breadwinner, full-time mom, and full-time provider for my aging parents. And when my dad passed away, I took care of that too.

And by the time I'd taken care of all the funeral arrangements, gotten him buried and my mom settled into her new life as a widow, my marriage finally unraveled completely. It was easier to focus on the new issue of impending divorce than it was to face the fact that my father was gone. I'm not sure I ever truly got the opportunity to grieve the passing of my father. And he deserved to be grieved over.

What I can tell each of you, though your stories might be different from mine, is that we serve an awesome God. In my complete brokenness, I was never alone, though it took time for me to call out to Him and ask for help. I can tell you that I'm healed and whole and that by His grace and mercy, I've been given a second chance to have a marriage that shines for the glory of God. We have happy, healthy, and whole children. But it didn't come without bumps in the road.

Whether you're still grieving your divorce or you're frustrated that your new blended family isn't quite what you thought it would be, let this book be the encouragement to press forward through the difficult seasons in your life.

2

DENIAL AND ISOLATION:

"Since this is an undeniable fact, you should stay calm and not do anything rash."
Acts 19:36

Denial

Our minds have an incredible system for processing and coping with tragedy. It doesn't mean we're weak, it means we're human. We're not normally conditioned to consume horrible events on a regular enough basis to dull us to devastating news.

Becoming desensitized, or having a diminished responsiveness to bad or adverse situations may sound like a benefit at times, but thankfully, we're more naturally inclined towards empathy.

Desensitization is a defense mechanism allowing us to turn off the humanity switch for the sake of getting the job done. As with everything in life, it comes with a cost. Trust me, the temporary pain of divorce sure beats the years of struggling to regain an ability to empathize.

If you're thinking how great it would be to avoid suffering the emotions associated with the pain of loss, please allow me to tell you differently. Like I said above, we're not naturally conditioned, but some of us have been professionally predisposed to consume the horrible.

It's much better to maintain the capacity to feel than to live numb. It's also the ability to feel that will help you move forward through the recovery and restoration process. During this initial phase, you may have tried or considered shutting off your emotional switch, but honestly, it's temporary and may only delay the recovery process. Various models of Christian counseling support that purposefully trying to suppress emotions creates an inner division instead of an inner connection[1].

Without the resistance against trauma, denial is your mind's accomplice. But, it's still just that—denial. Do you recall how you felt the first time your spouse told you they wanted a divorce? Maybe it had come up before, or was threatened so often the word divorce had lost its sting. But that last time, it was for real. However, the tragedy became reality, and you had to face it.

If you freaked, don't fret, very few people take this first bit of bad news head on. It's perfectly expected to experience denial. Even as the divorce papers are served and court dates are set, many people exist as hollow shells of who they were, without accepting the reality of divorce. They are in a word—*stuck*—or in denial.

Don't beat yourself up because of the way you responded during this stage. It's natural. When denial becomes unnatural it may encourage you to continue with unrealistic or unhealthy behavior. Sometimes risky choices are made in your state of compromised accountability, and the consequences aren't as clearly calculated before you make a leap you'd otherwise never consider. Most people fail to see the damage caused by denial until they're in too deep to climb out.

I'll interject a dose of my own reality at this point, and tell me if anything sounds familiar. My first marriage ended during my mom's battle with cancer. Fear of losing my mom was so powerful that I denied the real possibility of her death. In this, I also failed to see my marriage was on its own deathbed.

The irony was that professionally, I was emotionally stone cold, but when it came to my mom, I had no control over those suppressed emotions. Looking back, denial was the only tool I had to protect myself against her death and my eventual divorce.

Because my pride prevented me from asking for help, I didn't realize I was in denial. Or that it was okay to feel that way. After a while, I began to misinterpret my feelings as being out of control and abnormal. I knew I wasn't losing my mind, but the longer I suffered, the more I considered the possibility.

The extraordinary circumstances and the compounding worry over my mental state caused me to shut down anything to do with emotions—good or bad. By the time my mom passed away, I'd been divorced about two years. I still hadn't moved through the process of grieving divorce, or death. As a result, I continued making the worst possible life choices. They were a cry for help, but because I silently denied my pain, there was no one there.

Denial, although delayed, is an important benchmark for gauging your progress and protecting you during the transitional period between happily married and what happened.

No one wants to hurt, but when you consider the reality that a covenant you and your ex-spouse entered into with God has been desecrated, what else could there be but chaos? I didn't understand the spiritual investment or the eternal terms of the agreement at the time. All I knew was it was done and it was time to move on.

In retrospect, I was in denial about denial.

"Let no unwholesome word proceed from your mouth, but only such a word
as is good for edification according to the need of the moment, so that it will
give grace to those who hear."
Ephesians 4:29

Change is never easy, especially unwanted change; resisting change through denial quickly becomes a stumbling block to post-divorce recovery. If you've moved beyond this stage, or just entering the darkness, no one expects you to accept the news without adverse reactions. But this is also not the time to check out. There are still responsibilities that demand your attention. Yes, even the kids have to be picked up from school, and bills have to be paid. There are real life examples of people not doing these things. It really happens.

Isolation

"'The one who sent Me is with Me—He has not deserted Me. For I always
do what pleases Him.' Then many who heard Him say these things believed
in Him."
John 8:29-30

I've prayed with people who use the term "invisible" to describe their perception of loneliness. Rest assured, unless you're abandoned on an island without cell service or internet, you are not alone, and even then God is always with you.

Finding yourself single after divorce can create a confusion between lonely and alone. It's important to distinguish between the two. Because you're physically alone doesn't mean you're lonely.

Let's face it, you'll spend more time isolated once you begin to feel your feet touch solid ground. The sense of security is often accompanied by quiet reflection. Sometimes the solitude comes as a result of having moved into a different home and neighborhood. There will be the loss of mutual friends, the time your children will spend with their other parent, and the avoidance of social activities you once shared with your ex.

Gary Chapman's book *One More Try* reminds us that the road to happiness is not found isolated and focusing on your problems. It comes from pursuing God and focusing on His will.[2] Being alone can be used productively to bring time for prayer, reflection, and peace.

Feeling lonely may cause paranoia, rejection, and feelings of being unwanted or unworthy. God said it wasn't good for man to be alone. He created Eve as Adam's helper, and joined the two as one. This is a bond beyond any friendship, and a promise of God's desire to assure we are never alone. But God's idea of a helper wasn't one-night stands or rebound relationships. Please do not allow a fear of living alone drive you out of God's presence and into the arms of your next ex-spouse.

> *"Then the LORD God said, 'It is not good that the man should be alone; I will make him a helper fit for him.'"*
> *Genesis 2:18*

Breaking the suffocating grip of isolation has its roots at the very beginning of creation. Satan didn't bother with Adam until Eve entered the picture. Adam enjoyed a close, direct relationship with the Father, and satan understood he held no power in that union.

This is why satan hates marriages and uses isolation as a wedge while implanting discord of doubt and mistrust between two formerly loving people.

Have you ever wondered why satan does everything he can to get a couple in bed *before* marriage, and everything he can do to keep them out of bed *after* marriage? He does the most damage through sin and isolation.

> *"Can a man take fire in his bosom And his clothes not be burned?"*
> *Proverbs 6:27*

The isolation period is ripe for suspicion and paranoia. Formerly trusted friends, family, and allies, now use tools once shared for intimacy, as weapons for injury. Being alone, all alone, begins to consume you. Isolation even swarms over the most social or popular of people.

It's often the shame of failure and the desire to cut yourself off from the rest of the world that leads to the dark sensation of being alone. This same shame can stop you from moving through the short-term intention of isolation and into a chronic state of loneliness and depression. Reach out to someone trusted. Don't be a hero by trying to suck it up and power through this alone. You will lose.

In a quick note to other guys, I'm not sure why, but we like to think we're genetically coded to suffer in silence. Asking for help, or even dropping the facade of being macho in the face of adversity, is harmful to our ego. This isn't the season to "be a macho man," it's the time of life to be vulnerable and honest.

Carrying emotional junk around our necks is like a perverted badge of honor among men. Not all men of course, but enough of us to make broad sweeping statements about the state of man. Not to mention that I am a man who knows a bit about being male and unwisely silent in my suffering.

Men like to deal in areas of being respected and capable. To suddenly find ourselves invisible, irrelevant, or isolated terrifies us. I've always been a social person. While I was a cop, most of my friends were also cops. When my first wife and I split up, I found myself alone and not wanting to participate in activities we used to do together. I didn't want to hang out with the same couples we used to know. Eventually, I didn't want to leave the house unless it was for work.

The thought that all eyes were upon me caused me to feel less respected and capable. I'd failed as a husband and a dad, so what would my peers think of me? The best way to avoid their judgment was to avoid them. In hindsight, they weren't judging me, they were concerned and wanted to help, but later confessed they didn't know what to say. How I wished someone would have just asked. But in reality, the one asking about help should've been me.

Again, like most men, I have a need for respect, and I hated the feeling of powerlessness that accompanied isolation. I turned to what I'd always used to medicate my hurting in the past—physical sex. Consensual, non-obligatory, meaningless encounters meant I could stay at home and still experience a sense (although false) of being respected, and the fulfillment of being capable.

The end results spiraled me into even deeper pits of darkness and depression once the sex ended. Guilt over sexual sin piled onto the already vulnerable emotional state of being isolated, and I became engrained in a vicious binge-purge cycle. It's not just a man thing. For you, it may also be physical sex, alcohol, pornography, drugs, abuse or any number of unhealthy behaviors used to escape. What's important is to identify the fact that it's destructive and doing nothing to move you through the process toward healing.

My struggle was also increased by social and peer pressure. Law enforcement assumes a position as society's moral entrepreneur. I couldn't reconcile the sin I committed to numb my pain, with the outward façade of being society's savior behind a badge. It was all self-destructive behaviors, but wasn't I supposed to be stronger than that?

No. There was no way I, or we, are equipped to heal our own pain without the light of Jesus Christ. Isolating yourself from God's love will exponentially increase your irrational emotions and compound your guilt. You've got to remain plugged in to a caring body of believers, counselors or trustworthy family.

It took years and God's unrelenting grace before pulling myself from the shame of hell's destructive behavior. Being rescued now allows me to see with compassion, conviction, and an understanding of what others go through while in the muddied water of life after divorce and away from God.

People mistake connecting with others through social media as being sociable. Leah and I shudder looking at social media. I'm so thankful there was no such thing as Facebook, or even the internet, while I was in the pit.

We've all witnessed the train wreck—picture after picture of someone you know in a bar or out on an exciting adventure with an old high-school flame. Or maybe the blurred profile pics with beer in hand, hugging someone of the opposite sex. Those people are practically screaming, "*Single and Ready to Mingle.*"

They're not ready.

Just look beyond the façade of smiles and the loneliness of empty eyes. People going through Godless isolation are alone even in a crowded stadium. Loneliness isn't defined by an exterior collection of bodies. It's a condition of feeling emotionally abandoned. This dark emptiness is closely associated with pain and fear.

Pain and Fear

Remember when I shared the habit of saying things couldn't get worse, and they usually did? Well, a result of that suffer-resurface cycle was actual physical pain manifested by the constant stress my body was under.

I was a healthy adult, but it wasn't long until not only my heart hurt from absence, but physical aching set me into a constant state of concern. The difficult part about divorce and its effect on the mind and body is that we are used to getting upset and getting over it. The civil, legal process of divorce can take years to resolve, while the additional process of recovery may linger as well. Your natural being is not conditioned to endure years of agony without respite.

Maybe your team lost the game, or you didn't get the promotion at work. I was once told if you don't get upset by not getting the promotion, then you didn't want it very much in the first place. But we do get over it. Dr. Tony Evans reminds us that God is after a much greater purpose than experiencing pain. His book, *Divorce and Remarriage* is a favorite of Leah and mine[3].

Divorce is so much more than complaining about your team on Monday morning after a Sunday night loss. The bitterness, worry, stress, and unknown of divorce can linger for months, even years. Short of being Job, it rips at who you are—both physically and psychologically.

> *"In this you rejoice, though now for a little while, if necessary, you have been grieved by various trials."*
> *1 Peter 1:6*

Although it might have felt like the end of your world at certain times, it will pass if it hasn't already done so. And while you may not require medical attention, you should focus on a well-being solution to help deal with the stress until you've found yourself back on solid ground.

> *"For God gave us a spirit not of fear but of power and love and self-control."*
> *2 Timothy 1:7*

As kids, it was exhilarating to experience a jolt from the unknown. A scary movie, a crack of thunder while huddled next to momma on the couch, or a loud *Boo* when least expected. But fear of the unknown as adults, not so much. Fear is one of the factors that cause people to remain in unhealthy relationships or reconcile when they know it could be dangerous. It's an unfortunate example of "living with the devil you know."

While we accept that God did not give us a spirit of fear, it is often irrational thought or reaction running the show during this stage.

Leah and I both confess to respectively allowing feelings of fear to drive our otherwise rational characters.

Fear can also restrict your natural perception and force you into having tunnel vision where all of your options fail to clearly appear before you. This is similar to when you feel the very first raindrop, but don't realize it's part of a much bigger and threatening storm.

Fear is a powerful influencer. It can inject itself in many ways. While the feelings of fear are expected, if not addressed, they may persist or lead you down a path of complete despair. Hopeless people are vulnerable to suicide or attempts to end the onslaught of negative feelings of pain and fear if they feel they have no options.

Along with feelings of despair, suicide ideation[4] creates pathways for the unthinkable to become thinkable. While no one is prone to the feelings that nudge us toward that path, please do not ever hesitate to reach out to a tangible lifeline such as a parent, friend, counselor or preacher. You are not alone.

I asked Leah to share what she'd confessed to me about isolation. It's so personal that I was surprised when I read she was sharing this. It immediately told me she's super committed to this project and to you. I also know she's indeed found peace.

Leah's Story

I mentioned previously that I'd told my husband in 2007 that we were only married for the kids, but we had an unhealthy pattern to our relationship from the moment we met as teenagers, and we were great at masking the deep issues and moving forward with smiles on our faces.

I always think of Dory in *Finding Nemo* when she sings, "Just keep swimming, just keep swimming." That was us, except we were swimming in opposite directions and there was a school of sharks waiting to attack from the shadowy depth of the water.

In reality, my first husband and I never should have married. I knew he wasn't the right person for me within the first weeks of dating. But I was fourteen years old and didn't have the skills or strength of character at that time to call it off. I craved for someone to want me.

I grew up in a home raised by my grandparents. My mother had given me up for adoption to them when she was still a teenager because of drugs and other issues. My biological father had his own problems, and the last I remember seeing him was when I was around three. I knew the feeling of isolation and abandonment from my earliest childhood memories.

My grandparents were older, and though they provided a good home and I was able to get a solid foundation in Christ, it wasn't the kind of home where I felt I was anything more than a hindrance—nuisance —or mistake. Those words weren't spoken, but I felt them all the same, whether by looks or just general inattentiveness.

So, when I met my first husband at the age of fourteen, I was searching for anything or anyone to fill that void in my life—that need to not be abandoned or to know love from a male. I didn't fill the void with drugs or alcohol as some teens do (in fact, I wanted nothing to do with either because I saw what it did to my biological mother). I filled the void with the first male who showed attention to me, and I gave him everything I had to offer in hopes that it *would* fill that void. It didn't, and I regretted it immediately.

I was fourteen. I needed approval. I needed to feel loved and wanted. If I'd turned to Christ to fill the void as a fourteen-year-old kid I'd probably be telling a very different story right now.

It's funny to look back how things shape your life. I told you I'd been brought up in church and had a Godly foundation, but just before I started high school my grandmother had a falling out with the church. She'd been the church secretary and decided to resign. We didn't step foot in church again as a family after that.

I didn't have a youth group, a support system, or spiritual guidance.

Once again, I was left with no one but myself and my own choices —*isolated*. I was ripe for satan to get hold of, and it's truly a miracle I didn't spiral down a much darker path. At fourteen, all I wanted to be was an adult so I could get out of the house and get on with my life.

What I didn't have was strength. Not strength of character, not strength of purpose, and not the strength to believe in myself, that I had worth, and that God had a plan for my future that was much bigger than anything I could've ever dreamed.

Even as a child, I was a "peacekeeper" and not a "peacemaker." Peacemakers are blessed in the eyes of the Lord (Matthew 5:9), but peacekeepers walk on eggshells so no one gets upset. They avoid conflict and hide their emotions so as not to make anyone angry. They apologize to keep the peace, even when they have nothing to apologize for. Being a peacekeeper does nothing but build resentment and surface-level relationships.

I was a peacekeeper. Wouldn't it make sense to a child in my situation that keeping the peace would stop the people she loved from leaving? Or they might love her unconditionally if she never upset the balance of things?

My ex-husband had his own childhood demons to deal with, but we were an unstable compound from the start, and we were headed for an explosion. With as much courage as I could muster, my peacekeeping fourteen-year-old self tried to break things off with my seventeen-year-old boyfriend.

I had the intellectual capacity to know right from wrong, and also when a *situation* was "good" or "bad." What I didn't have was the strength to stand up to his self-destructive tendencies when I tried to call things off—*repeated* self-destructive tendencies, as I'd discover over the next years—or the ability to stand up to the peer pressure of disapproving friends. Because I would've been abandoned and isolated—*again*.

When you add sexual sin into the mix, it was a disaster waiting to happen. A fourteen-year-old kid—and I strongly emphasize the word kid because that's what I was—had no business engaging in or making those kinds of adult decisions. But I had parents who were uninvolved, my future husband wasn't a believer at that time, and I was looking for someone to love me. I learned if you look hard enough, you'll find it, even in the wrong places.

Fast forward almost two decades later and I found myself going through a divorce. I'd finally decided to file, and even though I was sick over the sin of it and what it would do to my children, I felt relief that the cycle was ending. On our Faithful Marriage Blended Family website, one of our contributors has a great article called *Relief Turned to Sadness*. Just like in the article, if my husband and I had a different relationship, and if either of us had truly been living in Christ, things might have gone differently. But because we weren't grounded in Christ and we'd let our problems build and manifest over almost two decades together, things went from bad to worse. And by the time the decision for divorce was made, the only thing I felt was relief. But there were a lot of other emotions I'd tamped down over the years just waiting to come to the surface. This leads to our next chapter on dealing with anger.

3

ANGER

"Be angry, and do not sin: Do not let the sun go down on your wrath, nor give place to the devil."
Ephesians 4:26-27

Ever wonder why the spouse is the first person the police question in a homicide? In my career, I've witnessed what uncontrollable anger can do.

Anger is okay—sin is not.

The reason we make this distinction is to reassure you that strong feelings against your ex-spouse or others who darken your door during this period are normal, but acting out or allowing others to lead you into sin is not advisable.

A trusted friend told us both that anger is not a sin, as long as you don't sin in your anger. Gary Smalley[1] further explains that anger is not sin, but it's a question of what you get angry about, and what you do in that state of anger that brings about sin.

Anger is a natural emotion. The intensity of that emotion must be kept in check. Ephesians 4:26-27 tells us anger is okay. In writing

Ephesians, Paul quickly points out that we should not allow anger to become such a controlling force that it causes us to sin. God understands we feel anger. We'd be grass eaters if it weren't for free will and emotions. But just to be clear, although God understands the feelings of anger, they do nothing in the way of glorifying Him or bringing you closer to Him.

"Human anger does not produce the righteousness that God desires."
James 1:20

Peacemaker Versus Peacekeeper

Learning how to express a healthy state of anger is something Leah struggled with and still struggles with. She explained in the previous chapter the difference between being a peacekeeper and a peacemaker. The problem with peacekeepers is it's impossible to make everyone happy all the time.

Even when she was right or being accused unjustly, she wouldn't say anything, just for the sake of keeping the peace. She's grown to understand the difference between the two and no longer stresses about the things "peacekeepers" worry about.

"Blessed are the peacemakers, for they shall be called the children of God".
Matthew 5:9

If you're a peacekeeper, it will only work for so long before resentment and anger build up and erupt in an unhealthy way. A spouse is going to know you better than anyone. That intimate understanding you two once shared is a great thing until the person becomes an ex-spouse. Then your buttons become their buttons, and that leads to a whole lot of mashing your buttons. Remember that those who anger you also control you. Make a pledge to reclaim self-control by refusing to step into their snare of anger.

Ken Sande's book, *The Peacemaker*[2], describes the differences between grasping for peace without the confidence of security and the active pursuit for developing an environment where peace is expected.

Sande's work is a great segue into this point about security. It's easy to claim both people should be able to say what's on their mind, but unless there is a safe landing pad for your expression, then most people won't willingly jump into shark invested waters. It's hard to discuss what makes us angry with someone who isn't engaged or concerned about what it was that made you angry. That was a stumbling block between Leah and me in the beginning. She was a rational talker and I wanted silence. I tried forcing peace through that silence, but through God's grace, I understood sweeping conflict beneath the rug accomplished nothing but more turmoil.

We're also familiar with the latter part of Ephesians 4:26-27 about not going to bed angry. How many nights have we huffed, scrunched the pillow, and rolled over in a furious knot before crashing into a fitful sleep?

On a lighter note, Leah and I, like most couples, like to be in physical contact before and while we sleep. It might be a hug beneath the covers, or a cold toe touching the back of her knee. Regardless, we like to touch, except for when I'm hurt or angry. Then she, claiming to be true to the command of not going to bed angry, will begin jabbing my leg with her own chilly toes.

Naturally, because I'm not happy with her, I scoot over. This is a double jab for Leah, because her love language is physical touch, and it's being withheld. Soon, I'm on the razor edge of the bed, and I imagine she's snickering at me. I either have to release the grip anger has over me, or fall off the mattress. The point is, it's not easy to just get over being mad. We work together to try resolving the issues so they don't fester. And so we also get a good night's sleep.

Processing Anger

I'll go ahead and bite the bullet on this example. Leah and I were talking with a Christian counselor who asked how I resolved anger. My first inclination was to correct him, because I don't get angry. Then I reconsidered the admonishment because, in fact, I do get angry. I just don't express it. Instead, I shut down, and Leah says she can see a complete physical transformation come over me. That's her cue to give me space to simmer and cool.

I'm usually pretty good at remaining calm, even in the most heated scenario. I know it's part of my demeanor and has been vital to responding professionally when a crisis was at hand. But honestly, I have no technique for managing my anger except to shut down.

So, as a well-skilled counselor does, he asked why.

I began praying for an answer. I knew there was something in my past that contributed to it, but when the life you live is the reality you know, why would you suspect something attributed to that? Eventually, God revealed my past through a pair of Christ-goggles. The truth hurt, but needed to be revealed.

I grew up in a very blue-collar home with my parents and us seven kids. It was the quietest, nine-person, Italian home you've ever seen. No one talked about anything. If someone got angry, they just stopped talking. When they got over being angry, they'd acknowledge the offender again. The problems came when one didn't get over being angry. My oldest brother left home angry. He didn't return for forty-three years.

Even when not angry, my dad didn't talk to me ever. We were both athletes...but there was no communication about sports. He was a high school coach and teacher, and I wanted to be a high school coach and teacher...but there was still nothing. We were the most similar in appearance and attitude, so we should've been two peas in a pod...*nada*. I grew up in silence. Especially when it came to God.

We never went to church as a family, and I knew nothing about God until I went out of state for college. When I did come to know Jesus as my Savior, my folks and I finally began to talk. They accused me of joining a cult. I shut down and walked out. God brought me back much later, but still no one talked.

My siblings and I continued the family silent treatment even after my mom died in 1999, and then when my dad passed in 2016. Now, most of us don't even acknowledge each other.

So to answer the counselor's question—*No*—I have no skill or experience in managing my anger. I did what my dad did, who did what his dad did, and so on down the line. We all just kept quiet. Anger may subside in my family, but it isn't resolved in silence. Now not only does the counselor understand, but so does Leah. And I finally understand too that I've been cursed by generational sin. Yes, being angry is okay, but my family not only went to bed angry, but we've harbored it over a hundred years.

Leah and I have committed to end respective family legacies of generational sin and start a new legacy for our children. My prayer is that none of them will ever go to bed angry. Oh, and my new answer about managing my unspoken anger is to confess it to Christ while my wife and I are in prayer.

"You shall not bow down to them or serve them, for I the Lord your God am a jealous God, visiting the iniquity of the fathers on the children to the third and the fourth generation of those who hate me..."
Exodus 20:5

You too will experience anger during your divorce recovery process. You can either post it publicly on social media, spend hours on the phone chewing on your friend's ear, or you can deliver yourself from 'its harmful clutches by giving it to God through prayer.

Talk straight with God. Don't pull any punches with Him. The anger, hurt, and suffering isn't going to surprise Him. He's a big God, and again, knows the condition of your heart. If you feel your anger is because of God, then please take your concerns to Him. We trust you'll soon understand that it wasn't His fault or actions that caused the offense, but it's important for you to see this for yourself.

We'll talk about forgiveness in a little while, but right now, you may be fighting to keep your head above water. The last thing on your heart is how to do a breaststroke versus a freestyle. But please focus on the source of your anger. It's unproductive to just be mad at everyone. Pinpoint the pain, pray through it and ask God to show you His heart over your circumstances. Moving through these phases requires you to allow the emotions to overcome you—not overwhelm you.

Cuts Both Ways

Anger has sure seemed to plant itself in a big portion of this book so far. We'd all be naive to pretend it isn't a major factor in the recovery process. So yes, it's natural and expected to have feelings of anger, but please remember that anger cuts both ways. It's easily projected at inanimate objects, strangers, friends, the ex-spouse, ex-in-laws, or worst case, your children.

Whether you were to "blame" for initiating the divorce or not, people will have their own opinions. Those opinions sometimes convert themselves into bitterly strong emotions. Your children aren't immune from these feelings. While they love you no less, swings of emotions may cause their anger to be directed at you, with or without justification.

Anger caused by divorce can be intense and last months, or even years. The pure stress from the constant state of unrest is enough to change a person's natural demeanor. In their unbearable anger, they may turn to actions such as verbal abuse and physical attacks.

Understanding that the grieving process is a natural evolution, and the sorting out of emotions is vital to progressing through the phases. The good and not so good news is that there's no "right" amount of time for getting through this tide of anger. But practicing active forgiveness is the spiritual breakthrough for handling the natural emotion.

"Then came Peter to him, and said, Lord, how oft shall my brother sin against me, and I forgive him? till seven times? Jesus saith unto him, I say not unto thee, Until seven times: but, Until seventy times seven."
Matthew 18:21-22

The apostle Peter was looking for the easy way to forgive, and possibly wanted a cutoff, so he could retaliate or reject his offender. But, Jesus corrected his assumption, and introduced an active, endless process of forgiving others. Jesus's example of seven times seventy doesn't mean we stop forgiving after four hundred and ninety times.

In His time, it was considered very "religious" to forgive someone three times. Peter doubled down plus one in an effort to avoid looking too unrighteous. Christ was quick to correct him that there is no limit to forgiveness. Isn't that reassuring that God doesn't wipe us out after a certain number of sins!

Just the Facts

It's crucial that you equip yourself to temper these emotional periods with information. While on duty, I've stood in living rooms where every piece of furniture had been demolished. The sparring spouses relentlessly quoted their versions of what they were certain the law said about divorce, community property, and custody. Almost 100% of the time they were wrong. Actors portraying attorneys on television make for good prime time drama, but lousy legal counsel.

Don't buy into the hyperbole. Take your time and make sure your attorney arms you with the facts, your rights, and all legal limitations as stated in the divorce decree and visitation of custody agreement. You may not be any less angry, but maybe you won't be easily manipulated by the button-pushing.

Post-divorce anger isn't always directed at the ex-spouse. Most Christians are uncomfortable admitting they are angry at their church or with their pastors. In Leah's Story, her experience with her home church during divorce proceedings surprised me the first time she shared it, but we've both learned that among women, it wasn't a rare occurrence.

Leah's Story

Anger is something I know a little about because I've spent a lot of years repressing it to keep the peace.

One of the biggest sources of anger for me during and after my divorce was the church. My ex-husband and I had been members at our church for twelve years. We went to Sunday school, and the kids had all been dedicated in that church. But we weren't involved in a community. If we'd been involved, people would've known we were married only on the surface. If we'd been involved and had close relationships, people would've known the marriage had been built on unhealthy patterns and sin.

I was on an insane travel schedule for book releases, and honestly, it was the best way I knew to escape my father's death and the impending divorce. I remember coming back from a rather grueling trip and going in to sit with my pastor. He told me two things that really got under my skin that day.

The first thing he told me was that he and his wife loved me very much and wanted to see me make the right decisions. Now, this is not a terrible thing to say under most circumstances. You're probably thinking I'm crazy for a statement like that to produce such rage inside me. But if you'll remember in the last chapter I talked about how I felt like I was drowning and all alone. And the honest truth is, except for Christ, I *was* alone.

So when the pastor said those words to me I became enraged (though I kept it inside because I'm a peacekeeper). For twelve years I'd been a member of that church and he was not only a pastor, but he'd been my Sunday school teacher for the previous two years. I was pretty sure he didn't even know my last name. And I knew without a doubt he didn't know the issues going on at home during the course of our marriage. But when he said he loved me and wanted to see me make the right decisions, all I could think was, "After all these years, you don't know the first thing about me, my husband, or my marriage. But you've decided you love me and care about me now that I've filed for divorce?"

The second thing he said was that everything I was working for was for nothing. He said, and I quote, "In a hundred years no one will remember you or your name." My place was at home with my husband and family. He asked me why I worked so hard, and the first thing I told him was that I wanted to leave a legacy to my children and grandchildren. But that wasn't the real reason.

The real reason was that I was running from my father's death and the unhealthy spiral of my relationship with my husband that started at the age of fourteen. But I didn't trust this pastor enough to tell him all the hurt that I was holding in. No one had ever cared about my hurt before, and honestly, I didn't believe he really cared when he said the words. It was just something pastors said, right? Otherwise, he'd have had some clue as to what was going on before he told me I needed to make right decisions regarding my divorce.

He followed up that conversation with a phone call while I was on a business trip. I remember being at a dinner with executives from a major book retailer, and it was almost ten o'clock at night. I was bone tired, and I saw my phone ringing on the table. It was the pastor, so I excused myself and answered the call.

This was a tough love phone call. The pastor told me I needed to get on a plane and get home. He said a lot of other things about "my" responsibilities, but I'd tuned out by that point. I was mentally and physically exhausted, and I kept screaming in my head, "You don't know us. You don't understand what happened. I don't want to "fix" this. It's over. Go give the other person in this marriage some tough love."

Because of his approach, I never trusted him enough to tell him some of the things that happened during my relationship with my first husband. To this day, I'm sure he still doesn't know, nor the congregation who were so quick to judge without knowing any facts. That's okay. It's not their business anyway. But I had to resolve my anger with this issue and forgive, just as I had to ask God to forgive me. I wasn't without sin, just like my ex-husband wasn't without sin. Just like the church isn't without sin.

But I was so angry. There's something about church iniquities that brings out a primal reaction in us. We expect different. We expect better. Because we know how Jesus suffered for us, and how his blood washed us clean. And we expect the church to have that same level of forgiveness. But the thing about the church is that its body is made up of people. And people are sinners. All of us. There's no exception to that rule except for the son of God.

It doesn't diminish our feelings where the church is concerned. In fact, I was angrier at that pastor than I ever was at my ex-husband. I'd learned to be numb with my ex-husband after the fight we had in 2007.

I came back home from that business trip and hunkered down with my children. We didn't go back to that church. I was angry at the pastor and the people. No one ever reached out. Everyone had their version of what happened in their head and that was that. It's like I ceased to exist.

I was not only isolated from my church family, but also from my actual family. They didn't know how to deal with me in a crisis. I was the one who always handled things. I couldn't fall apart, because none of them knew how to put things back together again.

It took me a couple of years to be able to speak words of forgiveness to that pastor because of my anger. And since my divorce, I've met with dozens of other women who speak of similar experiences. The statistics show that it's almost always the woman who feels she needs to leave her church after a divorce, not the man, even when it's the man's fault.

I was fortunate to turn to God after my divorce, even through my anger. But how many women never turn toward God again because of feelings of condemnation and isolation from the church? It's something we, as brothers and sisters in Christ, need to work on.

As for the words he spoke about no one remembering me in a hundred years or that my legacy means nothing, I have to disagree. Because Scott and I have drawn the line that generational sin will stop with us. And a hundred years from now, when our great-grandchildren are starting their own families, they can look back to us as the reason they know what a Christ-centered marriage looks like, and the reason they're raising their children to know and love God with all their heart.

That's a legacy worth leaving.

4

BARGAINING

"Rest in the LORD and wait patiently for Him; Do not fret because of him who prospers in his way, Because of the man who carries out wicked schemes."
Psalms 37:7

I have decades of experience in the realm of bargaining, although in my world it was called negotiations—most often hostage negotiations. Leah has handled the more traditional act of bargaining in the world of business. Whether it's professions or divorce, bargaining is about a need to gain or regain control.

Have you looked at your ex-spouse and thought they'd moved on just fine? Has it ever caused you to question that maybe they are happier without you, or maybe you were the issue all along?

It's natural in times of crisis, or desperation, to accept a position of self-blame and profess a willingness to change, even if you're in the right! Be aware of reconciliations that cost too much of who you are. Is any relationship worth existing as a façade? If your answer is yes, maybe check with Jesus for a confirmation before moving forward. Never negotiate or make decisions out of fear. Lawyers know this, and it's why deadlines and must respond by this date are always stamped in big bold letters at the top of most documents. I repeat, *do not respond in fear*.

As long as you feel there is equity in your position, not only is bargaining with your ex-spouse for a second chance a human inclination, but bargaining with God to give back your family is expected. Why wouldn't it be?

The key here is that you do whatever you feel led to do to gain the assured peace that you've given it your all. Is reconciliation preferable? In a redeemable situation it is. This is where you become more flexible to change and acceptance than you've ever been. Just don't compromise for the wrong reasons.

In my academic field of cultural anthropology, there's a term called *liminality*. Theorist Victor Turner[1] described it as a "betwixt and between." It's a state of being for whom a person once was and also who that person will become. There's usually an event or occurrence prompting the shift in personal perspective. Once you've passed through that threshold, you'll never be able to wholly return in the original, prior condition.

An example I use to better explain this theory is of the non-believer who accepts Jesus Christ as their Lord and Savior. Being saved is a truly life-changing experience for the non-believer. That would be the point of liminality, where their personal beliefs and perspectives shift to one of a believer seeking to know God's heart as opposed to the unrepentant sinner who only reveled in breaking it.

Unfortunately, the new creation in Christ will continue to sin, but their understanding of sinful consequences, confession, and restoration will never go back to that of an unbeliever. They now grasp repentance and forgiveness as part of their spiritual perspective. Even in their sin, they cannot return to a point prior to their perceptual shift. That seed is planted and will remain with them forever.

The reason I bring this up is that the act of divorce will change you forever. You'll be different—good different or bad different is up to you. Even if God blesses you with the truest love of your life, you'll always be a person who's been divorced. It doesn't have to define you, and that's why the consequences of these stages are important to understand for the health of any future friendships and relationships.

Once you've understood the consequences of divorce's finality, it's totally normal to try to change the position by asking your estranged or ex-spouse for a second chance, or promising yourself that you'll make changes, or even trying to cut a deal with God.

It's when we feel the decisions are no longer ours to control or influence that we move from an equal position of adversarial confrontation to a more submissive seeker of concessions. This is often a result of feeling helpless and vulnerable, and when we're most open to being compromised. On another note, ex-spouses can mysteriously become skilled at making you feel vulnerable.

Mind games, or "psy-ops," as we called it in police special operations, were often more effective than anything in a confrontation or bargaining position. For example, when negotiating with a bad guy who barricaded himself in a home, we'd cut off the electricity and water. It began to "mess" with their minds because normally no one likes being in a home without lights or water. If the bad guy conceded to our demand, we'd reward him with maybe a bottle of water. It was high-risk and lives were at stake, but it was a constant state of playing with their emotions until they became weary and we secured hostages or the bad guy's surrender.

Even without military or law enforcement experience, ex-spouses can become masters at "messing with your mind." Not because they've had specialized training, but because they know you better than anyone else. They know what buttons to push and dials to twist. Don't allow yourself to get drawn in for their mindless manipulation. Educate yourself. Consult your attorney, child caseworker, your kid's teachers, pastor, or whoever is responsible for intervening on your behalf.

Be aware that guilt factors into this phase like it does in so many other areas. The "what ifs" will dominate this period for grieving the loss of a marriage. We want to encourage you that this season, like everything in life, shall pass.

Don't give up on who you are for the sake of pretending to become someone you'll never be. I love the bible verse below. It's short and kinda light-heartedly blows the whistle on bargaining with a corrupt dealer.

"'Bad, bad,' says the buyer, But when he goes his way, then he boasts."
Proverbs 20:14

Guilt

Since guilt has been mentioned before, let's take a look at it as it's applied in the post-divorce recovery period. Guilt peppers itself into the mix whether the divorce was your fault or not.

We are naturally a self-assessing species. We invest too much time looking back at our faults and worrying what other people think of us. This can soon lend itself to sadness and even depression.

Kicking yourself a year after you failed to catch the carton doesn't put milk back in it. Are there opportunities to learn from our own mistakes? Yes, but now isn't the most productive time. Finding yourself divorced is a rough patch, so don't feel bad about deferring the learning lessons until you reach a healthier period. You'll make for a much better student of life later.

Your guilt may also resonate from the feeling that divorce is a sin. While there is debate over whether the act of divorce is a sin, the causes surrounding the initiation of divorce are usually rooted in sin.

This isn't a theological confrontation, but it is a good idea to identify your convictions regarding divorce.

Despite the legalistic logic, God hates divorce because He created marriage to mirror the intimate relationship He desires to enjoy with you. This is why satan was so quick and skilled in destroying the covenant between God and the first married couple in the Garden of Eden, and why marriage has remained under assault ever since.

Failing at a relationship created by God to mirror His love for us is a huge factor in carrying guilt. But God doesn't want you to tote it around like a wet burlap sack. Confess it and release it to Him. And, just in case you were wondering; yes God hates sin, but He loves the sinner.

"What therefore God has joined together, let no man separate."
Mark 10:9

With the burden of God's marriage model being broken, you are also carrying the weight of a suffering spouse, kids, family, and friends. The one-two punch of pain and guilt are mighty blows. Don't be surprised if they knock you onto your keister. God has a hand for you to grab onto. Don't allow your emotions, including your pride, to prevent you from reaching out for His loving lift.

I'll admit that I'm a pleaser by nature. I want everyone to get along and I worry that someone will be disappointed with an event whether I planned it or not. With that up front, the guilt I strapped to my spirit following my divorce was heavy. I mean really heavy.

For years after our divorce, my ex-wife and our son were all I worried about. I was so out of control that I allowed myself to feel guilty for every little thing that happened in their lives. It didn't even have to make sense before I started beating myself up over feeling guilty. That's the irrational part about it, there is nothing rational where satan's influence is concerned.

We can't stress how critical your relationship with Christ is at this time in your recovery from divorce. There is no bargaining position in that relationship. It is one of only surrender. Give yourself to Him, and cast your burdens at His feet. He will not abandon you.

"Now I rejoice, not because you were grieved, but because your grief led to repentance. For you were grieved as God willed, so that you didn't experience any loss from us. For godly grief produces a repentance not to be regretted and leading to salvation, but worldly grief produces death."
2 Corinthians 7:9-10

I have to tell you how proud I am of Leah for her open witness. She's an introvert by nature, so to see her words flow so deeply about her past and her hope has been a blessing to me. I've asked her again to share with you in Leah's Story.

Leah's Story

Guilt was a big stumbling block for me. I had four children, the youngest barely three years old and the oldest ten. I'll confess that they were the primary source of my guilt during and after my divorce.

The truth of it is, we all suffered a trauma, and the source of my children's trauma was based on decisions made by their parents. While they'd felt the fissure within the home the previous years before the divorce, to them, it was a normal way of living.

That's how I'd justify it to myself when trying to assuage my guilt. I'd tell myself that they were used to not living with both parents at the same time. If I had to travel, they'd stay with their dad and my mom while I was away. When I was home, their dad would go do his own thing. And we'd occasionally show up at the same place or event "for the kids."

I remember the day I told the oldest two about the divorce. I was immediately concerned for my ten-year-old. She tried to play it cool, saying, "Yeah, I figured as much." And then she made a couple of jokes and went on about her day.

Guilt slammed into me. Her response made me realize the long-term impacts divorce could have on her emotionally and relationally. Because when I saw that response from her, it was like looking in a mirror. That's how I handle trauma or events where there should be some kind of emotion. I shove it deep down inside, straighten my spine, and move forward.

What I've learned from experience is that emotions eventually catch up with you. Was my daughter on the same path for emotional destruction as I was?

Guilt.

My youngest son was the most traumatized of the four. He was still a baby, but he felt the impact of the divorce. My father had recently passed away, so through death and then divorce, he'd "lost" every male in his life. His father was still in his life, but custody schedules aren't the same as having a man in the house full time. That loss makes a significant impact on a boy.

Again. *Guilt.*

I watched the kids closely. I waited for grades to drop or rebellious attitudes to form. I looked for signs of the trauma and I waited for it to manifest. It was a daily worry, and I wondered how badly their dad and I had damaged them because of the choices we'd made.

But the choices were made, and they suffered the consequences of those choices. I asked myself constantly how I could make things better for them and what I could do for them. I wanted to see happiness in their eyes where there was despair and sadness.

Guilt.

I wasn't the kind of parent to fill the void with things or fun vacations, but I spent a lot of time and effort trying to make everything seem "normal." That's what I wanted for the kids—for them to feel like life was normal. I worked hard at it. And in my head I'd say, "See, this is exactly like it used to be. Even when we were married we weren't anything but a surface family so it looked good to people on the outside." That was my way of justifying my guilt to myself. My guilt was also intertwined with the stage of denial.

When I started focusing on Christ and turning to Him, with my hurts and with the kids', my guilt was laid at the altar along with everything else. Once the guilt was gone, we could truly focus on healing and being a family.

5

DEPRESSION

"Beloved, do not be surprised at the fiery trial when it comes upon you to test you, as though something strange were happening to you. But rejoice insofar as you share Christ's sufferings, that you may also rejoice and be glad when his glory is revealed."
1 Peter 4:12-13

By this point you've been through a tsunami of emotions. Now it's depression's turn to have its whack at you. I don't think it's an avoidable emotion, no matter what level of severity that's experienced. We've heard a few brave souls claim through pasted smiles that they never once suffered from depression. If there was absolutely zero degrees of depressed feelings in your spirit, then there may have been bigger problems than a failed marriage.

Your sinking emotions may have been a lingering sadness, melancholy, or clinical depression. Regardless of the degree, your feelings are warranted and a normal part of the process.

Take encouragement from 1 Peter. God says do not be surprised at the fiery trial. He knows what you've been through and what you're going to continue to experience. The big take away from this is God promises His glory will be revealed. Are there brighter days ahead? Yes, God made that promise to you.

I want to share this experience from my divorce to show just how easy what started out as a sadness morphed into something long-lasting and serious. I've always been an extrovert. While in law enforcement, I enjoyed the relationships and spent more time with other cops than I did family and other friends. But as I struggled and stumbled through my divorce, I began to feel a persistent sadness.

On top of the sadness I wasn't "getting over it," and compiling resentment against those who I thought moved away from supporting me through the difficult times. It was an irrational paranoia brought on by a deepening depression. I blew it off as a touch of melancholy, but when I couldn't shake it, I knew a deeper darkness had set in. I put on my best "I don't care" mask and headed into work. I know in my misery that I was tough to work for.

Without seeking help, it lasted for years. I'd fallen to a point where my first thought every morning was, "Why? Why should I go on another day?" Among my other duty weapons, I designated a revolver in my nightstand just for the moment when I could not think of another reason to get out of bed. I was crying out for help, but never once did I speak to anyone about it. I was too proud to show I was hurting. Some mornings, I wasn't even sure what kept me from pulling the trigger.

Once my reason for living returned to the rock of Jesus Christ, I knew there would be a tomorrow, and a day after that. Please, do not allow yourself to feel alone or invisible. Sadness, and even depression, may visit, but you have the authority in Christ Jesus to reject its destructive grip.

"Anxiety in a man's heart weighs it down (depression), but a good word cheers it up."
Proverbs 12:25

There are usually two types of depression associated with loss. Situational depression involves sadness and regret. It might be related to trivial or material issues such as a division of community property, or the unknown of where you're going to live once the house is sold, or even the cost of a divorce attorney.

This type of depression is often addressed with facts and information. Become active in educating yourself on the law and realities of divorce. This will minimize the stress of simply not knowing, which in and of itself causes symptoms of depression to deepen.

For the most part, divorce proceedings aren't like a pull of the slot machine. There are very structured civil laws that address everything from the amount of child support owed to who gets the family goldfish. Educate yourself and minimize the effects of situational depression.

The second type, clinical, is more serious and indicates a need for professional help. While it may appear more subtly than becoming sad over bad news, it's deeply personal and often misunderstood as another problem or illness. It often comes with the understanding that the divorce is a reality. This grieving is over the loss of what once was, and the earlier promises of what it might have been.

There are ways to maintain your balance once the divorce papers are signed and you're expected to re-engage in life. Like I'd mentioned earlier, the kids must be picked up from school and the bills must be paid.

The most important thing you should do after seeking a relationship with Christ is to give yourself some much needed tough-love. Drop the pride, ego or hardheadedness that has kept you from seeking professional help. You've allowed that limb to hang from the hip long enough. Get yourself better.

Hanging at the bar and crying in your beer or the two-for-one shots of cinnamon schnapps isn't going to cut it. Sure, people listen to your story, but after a while, a really short while, most friends and strangers grow weary. You need to find a solid support system to lean on. Divorce is tough. It's much tougher alone.

I used to talk about myself in terms of a grocery product. Kinda weird I know, but it helped me to visualize where I was in the divorce recovery process. If you had an unmarketable product as far as entering a new relationship, would you set it on the shelf?

Please make sure you are healed and whole before jumping into a new relationship. Rebound and second marriages fail at an alarming rate of sixty-seven percent. If you're not happy with you, no one else will be happy with you either.

Also, most of us go in looking for something in others that is missing from ourselves. The most common element is Jesus. We're looking for a partner who can be our Christ. Well, I think we can all agree that no matter how amazing that new fling appears, they are not, and cannot ever be, Christ.

And once you realize that this new love, just like the old love, isn't God that you're looking for, you'll lose that relationship to do what? Go find your next Jesus. This is why we are asking you to focus on the relationship with the one and only Jesus Christ before you try moving forward alone.

Another way to beat the blues is to maintain your health through diet and exercise. We've all seen the couch to marathon divorce survivors, but unless it's a lifestyle switch and not pounding the miles instead of the ex-spouse, the trend will be just that, a trend. Take advantage of this time to empower yourself. What's the definition of insanity? Doing the same thing over and over and expecting different results. Use this life gap between recovering and recovered to become the person you always wanted to be.

Avoiding Is Not Winning

Loss through divorce damages the hope you once had. The optimism doesn't shine as bright, but take heed, there is hope. Don't sit home waiting for life to happen to you. Be proactive during this season. Get or return to small groups in church, or find a church that suits you. Many people, especially women, do not return to the church they attended with their ex-spouse. To avoid the darkness of deep depression make sure you always have something to look forward to. Even if it's your next meal—find anchors until you're able to set sail.

While a depressed emotional state may stem from many causes, fear of the unknown is a major contributor. We talked about educating yourself earlier, but this is also the time to make a reality-based life plan. Just a few suggestions include:

- Understanding your financial picture
- Can or should you remain in the family home?
- Will you need to go back to work?
- How is your health?
- Who are your friends?
- Setting boundaries for interaction with the ex
- What will your relationship with the kids look like?
- Who do you want to be at the end of this?

There Is Hope

"Hope deferred makes the heart sick, but a longing fulfilled is a tree of life."
Proverbs 13:12

As we learn by leaning into Christ, there is hope. It's been a long road, and one you never expected to travel while first falling in love. But the reality is, you've made it. Let's start looking for the positives. You'll come through the negatives and still be standing, so leave that where it belongs. Look ahead to what can become the you God wants you to be. Everything in the recovery process eventually dovetails into your next season of life; Acceptance.

Leah's Story

I know depression well, but not because it was something I was used to. I'd never once experienced depression before my divorce. I always prided myself on being a resilient, stubborn woman who could weather the storms of stress, no matter how bad it got, and keep moving forward. It turns out that ability manifested because of the pain I'd been suppressing my entire life.

Then my father died. It was like someone had punctured my heart, and from that puncture mark, tiny fissures began to crack and spread through my body. Then my marriage finally came to an end and the cracks turned into canyons. There was no patching or piecing the wounds back together, because the cracks formed faster than adhesive could be applied.

The stress and overwhelming emotions were getting to the point where I couldn't ignore them like I'd always done. I stopped eating, and when I did eat, I could only take two or three bites at most before it came up again. I was at an unhealthy weight—a size zero—for my five foot seven frame. And all I wanted to do was sleep all the time.

Just because my personal life was in crisis didn't mean my work obligations stopped. It was worse when the kids went to visit their dad, and I was alone. I still had work deadlines, but I couldn't stay awake to get them done. I was sleeping sixteen to eighteen hours a day, I weighed next to nothing, and I looked like a fragile shell of myself.

When I told Scott about this period of my life, one of the things I said was that I stopped hearing God. I prayed, but there was part of me that was so numb that I completely shut Him out. He never left me, but I felt utterly alone. Because of me. Not because of Him.

Breaking down completely in my prayer closet was how I started to heal. I did ask God why. I did vent my anger, frustration, and bitterness. And I did bring my sins to the cross and ask forgiveness. It's funny how you can hear Him when you submit and listen.

Depression is something I recognize now. I've experienced it. I've survived it. And there have been moments in life when I've felt the dark edges of depression creep in. The first thing I do is go into prayer. The second thing I do is ask Scott to pray for me too. There is healing in prayer.

6

ACCEPTANCE

"Not that I speak in regard to need, for I have learned in whatever state I am, to be content: I know how to be abased, and I know how to abound. Everywhere and in all things I have learned both to be full and to be hungry, both to abound and to suffer need. I can do all things through Christ who strengthens me."
Philippians 4:11-13

This is a difficult stage. Acceptance shouldn't necessarily be associated with being happy or excited to move on. Oftentimes, acceptance is the most difficult part, and in no way is achieving it even guaranteed. It's best to think of it in terms of how it's described in Philippians 4:11-13—being content.

Acceptance may include withdrawing from the situation and those associated with it. Yes, it's a tough time, especially for the children who are more confused than anyone involved. This doesn't mean you are or aren't still having struggles. It's important to make that distinction. Acceptance is finally having the ability to sit quietly and claim a sense of calm over the tumultuous proceedings.

Processing through the recovery stages of divorce is deeply personal and unique to you. While no one can help you avoid any one of the stages, they might make it more tolerable. It is possible that avoiding a stage will only ensnare your heart within it and prolong the healing process.

I shared that I married immediately after my first divorce was finalized. It was a total rebound and lasted about one and a half months. No way was I content in my life, as I'd made a mockery of the recovery process. I was still in a deep depression because I'd ignored the stages of recovery. Struggling endured because I wanted to maintain the tough guy facade that nothing bothered me. I clung to the first woman who paid any attention to me as an escape from the stages of grieving a true loss. As you now know, that decision exponentially compounded my problems.

Why did I crumble? Because although God was reaching out, even stretching over to lift me up, I chose to belly crawl to the self-pity party and avoid Him. It ended up costing me valuable time and deep despair in prolonging the process of working through the loss of divorce.

The most productive action you can take is to understand what it is that you'll be facing, and then brace yourself as you allow the experience of reality as grief washes over you. You can't hide from it, but you *can* survive it.

Forgiveness

Leah and I also want to add—and it's possible that we've waited a little late to discuss it—but forgiveness is absolutely required. Now wait a bit before wagging your finger and saying out loud, "No way, Scott."

As believers, God wants us to have the capacity to forgive, just as He does. God makes it clear in Matthew 6:14-15 and Mark 11:25 that we are to forgive those who trespass against us, or accept that we will not be forgiven.

"For if you forgive other people when they sin against you, your heavenly Father will also forgive you. But if you do not forgive others their sins, your Father will not forgive your sins."
Matthew 6:14-15

Forgiving others is sometimes one of the hardest things to do. But forgiveness isn't for the offender. It's for you. And forgiveness doesn't mean you approve or accept the actions that hurt you, and it doesn't mean you have to reconcile the relationship or even make an attempt at putting a smile on your face.

In fact, it's not even necessary to speak the words of forgiveness to the one who aggrieved you. But speaking the words out loud, even if in private, creates a healing effect in your heart. Maybe not that first time, or the twentieth time, but you are preparing your spirit to be healed through the faithful words from your lips.

We're sure you've felt like we have too about forgiving others. It's like, "Why should we let them off the hook?" Trust us, they will be held accountable for their sins, but not by you. Sin is violating God's law, so for you to try to exact justice on the sinner is, in effect, denying God His right to discipline the sinner for violating His law. Who do you think is better at serving justice? You or the Creator?

"Beloved, never avenge yourselves, but leave it to the wrath of God, for it is written, 'Vengeance is mine, I will repay, says the Lord.'"
Romans 12:19

I'm not sure about you, but that verse kinda makes me smile a bit. Instead of fuming for days or decades over what they did or didn't do, or what you thought or should've known, try forgiving them. God will take care of the rest. You don't have to reconcile with them either. God gives you the authority to no longer be victimized by a lingering relationship. Mark your boundaries and abide by them. It'll simplify your life.

One of our kids had forgiven their sibling for something hurtful they'd said. Well, as kids go (and adults) the aggressor said it again. Our youngest asked why he should keep forgiving when they were just going to keep calling him names. He had a point, but he was also looking for implied consent to retaliate.

Look at Peter's interaction with Jesus. He tried to test his friend by suggesting seven times forgiveness.

"Then Peter came to Jesus and asked, 'Lord, how many times shall I forgive my brother who sins against me? Up to seven times?' Jesus answered, 'I tell you not just seven times, but seventy times seven!'"
Matthew 18:21-22

You cannot stop forgiving someone any more than Jesus can stop loving you. Can you take positive action to prevent the continued abuse? Sure you can. What did the youngest do? He reported the harmful taunting to us, and we as parents took "vengeance" on the one who should've known better. It's the same model God wants us to follow. But the youngest also made sure to stay out of his older brother's room and thus avoid the abuse. See, it works on all levels.

Remember, forgiving sets you free from the person and the act that hurts. Leah and I were in prayer one morning and God laid the act of forgiveness on both of our hearts. We understood that we must actively seek out those in our life, and even in our past, who have caused pain or spurred on generational sin, so we can forgive them. We became aware of pain we still carried because of our parents. It took a lot of deep, soul-bending prayer to forgive, but when we did, we were both set free. It was a glorious liberation.

Brighter Days

We know this may seem like an insurmountable task, but while it may feel like a death, it's actually an opportunity to begin anew. The foundation you lay for this journey is important. Unless your path is lit by the light of Christ, you may wander back into the darkness along yet another rocky trail.

We've been there, and it was only by the merciful forgiveness of God that Leah and I were blessed in finding each other. Divorce is traumatic, and whether you pretend it doesn't matter or you're shattered to pieces, it has an effect on you.

The stages discussed above are basically what you can expect to encounter. If you've moved beyond them, then they're a good reminder why proceeding forward with caution is so significant. But the key is that you move forward to brighter days.

We love what Jeremiah 29:11 says. It promises us that God has us in mind, and that He has it all under control. No matter how bad your divorce is or was, please cling to the eternal promise of hope that only God can offer.

"For I know the plans I have for you, declares the LORD, plans for welfare and not for evil, to give you a future and a hope."
Jeremiah 29:11

Acceptance isn't a word I think I would've associated with Leah at one time in our marriage. I've seen what forgiving me and forgiving others has done in her life. She has found peace in the Lord, and now being content for her looks more like pure joy. I'd love to have you read what she has to say about it.

Leah's Story

Acceptance...since we're being totally honest with you about the things we've gone through and learned, I'll tell you acceptance took a while for me. In fact, Scott and I had been married more than a year before I really went through the final stages of healing and forgiveness from my first marriage.

Not because of regret, guilt, or any of the other stages we've talked about thus far. But because of forgiveness. Or, in my case, the lack thereof. I could feel the bitterness and anger growing inside of me over hurts from my first marriage. Hurts I never shared with my ex-husband. I also had anger toward ancillary forces that I was dealing with in regards to my first marriage and divorce. And I clung to that anger and bitterness. Because I had a *right* to those feelings.

I wonder how many times God closed his eyes and shook his head at me during this time. Not forgiving was holding me back from freedom. It was also holding me back from what I needed to put into my marriage with Scott. How unfair was that to him, to still harbor that bitterness and anger towards my first husband? I was holding on to anger from when we'd first met at the age of fourteen. That's a lot of years of pent up resentment.

I can tell you I know exactly what I'm talking about when I say forgiveness is a necessity for healing. Forgiving others and asking God to forgive me was an immediately freeing action. The best analogy I can give is that God took turbulent, violent waves and turned it into a calm sea.

Letting go of the anger of that past let me focus on the promise of my future with Scott and the importance of our marriage. It gave me peace and hope. And it prepared my heart to be able to keep forgiving others, because God knew there were some rough spots coming in my life where I would need to extend grace and forgive. The old me might have handled those situations very differently. But the new me, the changed me, was able to extend grace and forgiveness and heal.

I thank the Lord every day for that lesson in forgiveness.

7

F-A-I-T-H RECOVERY MODEL

How do you get from point A to point B?

Without a roadmap, you may never get out of the driveway. Do not leave your divorce recovery to chance, or in anyone else's hands. You must build a path that bridges the life you just lost to the living you now desire. It's easy to sit on the muddy bank and wallow in the mist, but that isn't the life Christ has for you.

It's funny, but hindsight really is 20/20. It took me years to find my way to point B. I wish there'd been someone or something to simply call out, "Hey Scott, let me mentor you on how to get yourself out of this mess." It would've saved me years of wrong turns, hardship and heartache.

Sure, I knew God's Word, but handing a new believer a Bible and saying, "See ya next Sunday," wasn't any more the answer than what a dog would do if he actually caught the car he was chasing. I needed a seasoned coach to equip me with the realities of what I was factually facing. Theory is one thing, experience and practical application are another. Leah and I understand that the key element of life experience is why God called us to write this for you. Although we were sure He was talking to more learned scholars, in fact, He wanted the once broken to help heal others.

At the time, I wasn't prepared to enter into a holy marriage covenant with my first wife. I sure wasn't equipped to handle the reality of divorce. Possibly worst of all, I had no clue what life on the other side of divorce held for me. I was raw and waiting to be devoured. And devoured I was, indeed.

Leah and I have both been there. Neither of us are proud of having been divorced, but we no longer walk around in shame because it doesn't define us. Nor does it define you. We've been moved to mentor others like us. Therefore, we set out on a quest to discover a faith-centered structure based on our personal experiences, best practices, and ultimately, God's word. We needed a tangible roadmap to ensure the lineage of divorce was over and the promise of a legacy of love and life together was ensured.

Our practical F-A-I-T-H Recovery Model is offered as a structured guide to help you progress through the realities of life once you've experienced divorce, and while you grow more confident in your walk with Christ. The F-A-I-T-H model is your path from recovery to romance during the transitioning seasons from loss to victory.

In times of crisis or high stress, it's best to keep things simple. The F-A-I-T-H Recovery Model is just that—simple. But, as important, it's practical and it works. Let's take a look at the step-by-step process that you will follow toward restoration.

Forgive

"For if you forgive others for their transgressions, your heavenly Father will also forgive you. But if you do not forgive others, then your Father will not forgive your transgressions."
Matthew 6:14-15

Let us state the obvious; Recovery begins with forgiving. God makes no bones about it. If you forgive others, God will forgive you. If you do not forgive others, God will not forgive you. You will not progress one inch toward recovery with the burden of unforgiveness strapped around your spirit.

Aim

"God did this so that they would seek him and perhaps reach out for him and find him, though he is not far from any one of us."
Acts 17:27

Recovery requires a laser-focused effort to connect with those things in your life that eliminate strife, offer hope, and ensure stability. Focusing on your relationship with God is the singularly most important action you will take toward reclaiming peace in moving forward.

Inspect

"Let us test and examine our ways, and return to the LORD!"
Lamentations 3:40

Recovery requires taking a realistic inventory of your life. Understanding what once was and what will no longer be, is a positive step toward accepting that you are no longer living a life of loss. Use this inspection to count your blessings as the foundation for your victorious future.

Transition

"For I know the plans I have for you, declares the LORD, plans for welfare and not for evil, to give you a future and a hope."
Jeremiah 29:11

Recovery leads you into a vulnerable season of transitioning from bud to bloom. People find themselves in the stage of feeling more confident, yet carrying around insecurities and pain from their past. Seasons of transition hold as much risk as they do reward. But without them, we cannot progress forward toward recovery.

Heal

"LORD my God, I called to you for help, and you healed me."
Psalm 30:2

Recovery is an active process of progressing toward being healed. Healing comes in many shades, but arriving at the point of forgiving, proclaiming Christ, realistically understanding your circumstances and having moved through a season from defeat to victory are keys to knowing true spiritual healing. There can be no legacy of victory while shackled to a past of pain. Healing is your hope.

8

SPIRITUAL GROUNDING

We want to shift gears for a moment and talk about prayer as an anchor in the storm and a beacon for the future. Many people recovering from divorce suffer months and maybe years without understanding what they were experiencing or why. Left unknown, people can begin to mold into a blame posture whether justified or not, they accept fault and consequences. This is where prayer comes through. There is no blame, only truth.

It's funny to hear kids, and oftentimes adults, begin their prayers with a personal introduction; "God, this is Timmy..." or "God, I'm not a religious person..." Guess what? God's got you covered. He fashioned you in the womb. He breathed a soul into the life your mom carried around until birth. He created you!

God knows who you are, and He sure knows how frequently you talk to Him. He also doesn't want you to be a "religious" person. God wants you to be you. He seeks a personal relationship with you, and that isn't done with rituals or recited chants. It's a loving relationship built through the good times and the bad. It's a trust established by talking with Him.

Broken?

Did divorce break your heart? Did you cause the conditions leading to your divorce and now you're burdened by the shame of guilt for destroying your family? God knows this. He grieves at your pain, but He is patient for your return to Him. He has a plan for your life and there is joy in sharing that with you.

You will not discover God's desire for your life through a sign or miracle. You will come to know God's desire for your life through prayer. Once you actively seek Him through prayer, God will place the unmistakable desires of your life, deep inside your heart.

Eventually, your emotions will stop swinging like Tarzan through the jungle. But maybe now you're still unable to get through an entire conversation without wanting to smash, squeeze, or shout. Good news is, you're almost there. At least you're coming out from your hidey-hole to re-engage in life.

Call On Him

How often have we cried out to Jesus in our despair? How often have we followed through with seeking Him once the crisis has passed? While there are times for crying out in the moment, the process of seeking God's desire for your heart is much more than a one-time query.

> *"Trust in the LORD with all your heart and lean not on your own understanding; in all your ways submit to him, and he will make your paths straight."*
> *Proverbs 3:5-6*

God has been there during the divorce and in the recovery from it. We usually keep God at arm's length until we need a shoulder to cry on or a fist to rattle at. Walk with Him always instead of on a desperate occasion and see the wonder of His love.

You are in a restart season of renewal. It's like having freshly tilled soil, and an opportunity to plant a new, more beautiful bounty. Unless you seek God's desire at this point, you'll most likely toss in more weeds and chipped rocks. And to no surprise, you're back on the same sand that just shifted beneath you.

There are an unlimited number of unknowns surfacing in your life right now. The natural reactions are to either hide from all of them, or to snatch the first one out of thin air. That usually ends up entering what we call rebound marriages. Please don't do it.

Take this time to seek your true love—God.

Trust me on this one. I have the T-shirt, and the consequences to prove it. Practice the patience you preach. After my second marriage, God mercifully told me to be still. Actually, He told me to immediately stop doing what I was doing. His will was for me to stop panicking over being alone and worrying about the if, when, or where would I find love. It was almost twenty years before meeting Leah, but amen that He kept me in His mercy and grace.

God Wants to Bless You

Praying is a precious action. You ask God for something and you don't get it. You stop praying. That wasn't seeking God's will. That was seeking a Santa Claus. Your pursuit of God should be to know His heart through prayer. Once God gives you the desires of your heart, He will provide the way for His will to be done.

God is crystal clear about wanting you to live an abundant life. We're unsure where the material peasant's life became biblical chic, but it's the heart of the person, and not the bank account that defines spiritual abundance.

If you are like I was, the question I wanted answered most by God was would I be alone the rest of my life. Of course, it was driven by fear. After my second divorce, I felt broken and unfit to be loved. It wasn't until I began to pursue God in earnest that I experienced the true joy of a spiritual relationship. Once I was able to love myself, God knew I was ready to love someone else. Only then did He place His desire for remarriage in my heart.

One of our hopes is to inspire you to follow love once the time is ordained. How will you know? If you've pushed to know God's will for your life, and your will has meshed with His, you will know without a doubt when the time for love is right. How can we be so sure? God's desire for your joy is clear.

"Until now you have asked nothing in my name. Ask, and you will receive, that your joy may be full."
John 16:24

We're asking you to take this season of your life to slow down. If the divorce wasn't your doing, then your life got stuffed in a blender and set on high speed. Court dates, attorney visits, life changes and relationships ending were all factors keeping you relatively out of control of your own life.

Guess what? You are back in charge. It's either exhilarating or terrifying, but it's your choice. This is your time to redeem the quality of life diminished by divorce. Look what Solomon wrote in Ecclesiastes about seasons in life. There are many and they come and they go. Don't beat yourself up over the one that passed.

"To every thing there is a season, and a time to every purpose under the heaven:
A time to be born, and a time to die; a time to plant, and a time to pluck up that which is planted;
A time to kill, and a time to heal; a time to break down, and a time to build up;
A time to weep, and a time to laugh; a time to mourn, and a time to dance;
A time to cast away stones, and a time to gather stones together; a time to embrace, and a time to refrain from embracing;
A time to get, and a time to lose; a time to keep, and a time to cast away;
A time to rend, and a time to sew; a time to keep silence, and a time to speak;
A time to love, and a time to hate; a time of war, and a time of peace."
Ecclesiastes 3:1-8

Is God Listening?

Can you petition God to listen to you? Yes, you can and you should learn to pray with expectancy. You are asking for a supernatural miracle from the Creator of existence. You cannot approach Him with uncertainty like hoping the lotto will strike lightning with your pick six numbers.

If you seek God's will as it was placed in your heart, then what you ask of Him through prayer is pleasing and already known to Him. You should be confident in the expectation that He will deliver.

In my first year as Chief of Police, my pastor, Ronnie Melancon gave me a copy of Mark Batterson's, *The Circle Maker*[1]. He stressed my administration's real battle in combating the city's problems was a supernatural one, and had little to do with crime. He assured me that prayer was going to make the difference.

It confused me because I was an experienced police commander with advanced academic degrees and a national subject matter expert on predicting and eliminating crimes. Fighting criminals was my mission, not the city's supernatural issues.

It wasn't long before I understood the reality of my position. Not as a Chief of Police, but as a believer in Christ. The onslaught of illegitimate and demonic indwelled accusers was relentless, but my pastor had taught me how to armor up with the defensive protection, and the offensive weapon for victory—Prayer.

Prayer was the answer, and Batterson's book about praying with confidence and expectancy was vital to my successful administration. Little did I know at that time, God was planting the seeds of learning to lean on my prayer life to realize His will for me. Still curious about the idea of just asking through prayer? Let's look at 1 John:

"And this is the confidence that we have toward him, that if we ask anything according to his will he hears us. And if we know that he hears us in whatever we ask, we know that we have the requests that we have asked of him."
1 John 5:14 and 15

All you have to do is talk to Him. God loves you. Don't be afraid to open up, like you would to a trusted friend. Too many people fear God is just waiting to zap us for any mistake. We're not kids anymore. He is a good Father, and goes out of His way to love us. God truly adores you, and wants you to have a very close relationship with Him.

Your Heart

God knows the intentions of your heart. He will remove the hurt, the hate, and the helplessness you feel if you allow Him to do so. How does He know? Because you've cried out to Him regularly and in all circumstances. God is not a spiritual 9-1-1 operator. He wants your shout out in the good times as well as the bad. Give it a try. Anywhere. Anytime. Just talk to Him. About what? About anything.

How about you try this as a starter? Read the ice-breaker paragraph below out loud, and then set our book down for a moment to listen for His reply, or if you feel comfortable enough, just keep talking to

Him. He hears you from your core, and He loves to have you reach out to Him. We'll catch up once you've chatted with God for a while.

"God, I'm reading a book that's talking about knowing Your desire for my life. It says I should talk to You about what's going on in my life. I don't know what to say or how to even begin a conversation, so I'm going to tell you what's on my heart—the joys and the burdens. I'll trust You with my words, and trust You to show me how to talk with You. I'll confess, this is a little weird, but I trust that You know my heart. I'll start at the beginning..."

"Therefore, if anyone is in Christ, the new creation has come: The old has gone, the new is here!"
2 Corinthians 5:17

New Creation

We love what 2 Corinthians says about being a new creation and that the old is gone. It's what has sustained us both in our darkest days. The promise that we are new in Christ and redeemed means we are not condemned to remain that person who caused the divorce or the person left behind in the wake of it.

There are a few truths we've experienced and want to share with you. Some you may recognize, while others you may have already visited or are about to encounter.

We use the term "solid ground" with relativity. Once you've processed the various stages along the recovery from divorce, there comes a period of calm where solid ground may be found. While there are no assurances you will totally get over the emotions associated with divorce, you will move forward if you focus your recovery on Christ's word.

Here're a few things to consider in drawing closer to blessed restoration through God.

Seek First a Relationship With God

While this is life-changing advice, it is also like telling a teenager to go find a job. Neither the job seeker nor the Christ-seeker is given the information needed to be successful in their quest. Chances are, neither one will accomplish their goal.

What does a relationship with God look like? How can a mere human have a true relationship with the Creator of existence? Is it even possible, and does God really care?

If you sincerely want to experience the newness of a relationship blessed by God, then you must seek this relationship above all others. Many people are afraid to go all out and be seen by their peers as Jesus Freaks or Holy Rollers. A Christlike vision through a Godly lens will remove those carnal worries within your spirit.

This is about you. Do not allow others to steal your reward because of the gossip over why you divorced or which one of you caused it. Get yourself right with your Maker and you shall know peace over and beyond the drama created by others. Introduce yourself to the One who loves you more than that ex-spouse ever claimed to have.

Your relationship begins the instant you confess your need for Him. Crying out to Jesus is more important than texting your best friend. It won't be the hours of random gossip that prepares you to trust and love again. It will be the confession, repentance, and the opening of your heart to receive Jesus as your Lord and Savior.

You can know God on a one-on-one level. Look back to the Garden of Eden before sin was first introduced. Adam and Eve knew God very intimately. He walked and talked with them in the garden.

"And they heard the voice of the LORD God walking in the garden in the cool of the day: and Adam and his wife hid themselves from the presence of the LORD God amongst the trees of the garden."
Genesis 3:8

It was sin that separated them from direct access to God, but it's through Jesus Christ that we are forgiven and may know Him once again. To know God also means including Him in every aspect of your daily live. We do this by praying, reading His word, and seeking His will.

God wants so badly for you to draw close to Him, that He left us a helper to serve as our Counselor. The Holy Spirit will guide you in your quest to know God in a genuine relationship.

"If you love me, you will obey what I command. And I will ask the Father, and he will give you another Counselor to be with you forever—the Spirit of truth. The world cannot accept him, because it neither sees him nor knows him. But you know him, for he lives with you and will be in you."
John 14:15-17

This is the part of the conversation where people tend to step back. Some think it's either too complicated, or once the Holy Spirit is introduced, they fear it's a form of mysticism. Again, it's okay to doubt. He's big enough to take your questions and answer your concerns. The Holy Spirit is God, and remains with us daily to clear our paths back to the Father. The Holy Spirit will help you in your times of doubt and cheer you in your times of victory.

"Then he said to me, 'This is the word of the LORD to Zerubbabel,' saying, "Not by might nor by power, but by My Spirit," says the LORD of hosts."
Zechariah 4:6

Benefit of the Doubt

Do you recall the story of the disciple, Thomas? How could you not? His nickname has stuck with him throughout history. Doubting Thomas wasn't the only disciple to question the resurrection of their friend and savior, but he was the one who spoke it.

Despite others witnessing the return of Jesus after His crucifixion, Thomas continued to doubt their testimony. After all, Jesus died on the cross. Thomas did not sin against God for his questioning. Instead, Jesus came to Thomas and offered him to experience Christ in a very personal way. We say offered because Thomas, just like you, have the freedom to experience Christ or not. No others had requested to touch the nail-scarred hands, but that was because each had their own method of processing faith.

> *"Now Thomas, one of the Twelve, was not with the disciples when Jesus came. So the other disciples told him, 'We have seen the Lord!' But he said to them, 'Unless I see the nail marks in his hands and put my finger where the nails were, and put my hand into his side, I will not believe.' A week later his disciples were in the house again, and Thomas was with them. Though the doors were locked, Jesus came and stood among them and said, 'Peace be with you!' Then he said to Thomas, 'Put your finger here; see my hands. Reach out your hand and put it into my side. Stop doubting and believe.' Thomas said to him, 'My Lord and my God!' Then Jesus told him, 'Because you have seen me, you have believed; blessed are those who have not seen and yet have believed.'"*
> *John 20:24-29*

Faith is the key. Even in doubt, trust God and have faith that He is with you. All you have to do is make the effort to pursue Him. It's not an overnight pill, but you will know that your life is changing and being remolded. Have faith that God wants what is best for you. He is a God of second chances, and that also includes finding and keeping new love.

Seek Christian Fellowship

Have you noticed your circle of friends shifting? Divorce not only affects you and your family, but also the associations you and your ex-spouse shared. It's not high school, but picking sides is inevitable. Don't be surprised if you find yourself blocked on Facebook and other social media pages.

It's all rather silly when you consider what's important. Leah shared that a close friend actually requested she un-friend the woman he'd broken up with so he wouldn't inadvertently see his ex's posts in Leah's Facebook feed. She unfollowed him instead.

While you may feel most comfortable falling back in with the old gang—your friends from high school, college, the night club scene, or the gym to name a few—they'll never have your spiritual healing in mind. We run backward because like that tattered pair of jeans, they're comfy, but not complete.

Socially, we're the aggregate of the five people closest to us. Take a look at your friends. We don't mean your co-workers, gym partner or acquaintances. We mean your ride-or-die friends. Are they all in for your recovery? If not, you need new friends who aren't invested in reminiscing about the past, but are laser focused on proclaiming an incredible future.

Look at Exodus 14:10-12 below, and tell us if this sounds familiar. God's people begged to be freed from the Pharaoh's oppression in Egypt. Finally, Moses was lifted up to deliver them out of bondage and slavery.

But as life would happen, things got a little difficult once they escaped into the unknown. Then, just like the ex-spouse, temptation or fear of the uncertain, Pharaoh came after them with a vengeance. He wanted to drag them back into slavery.

Instead of standing for what was right with Moses and trusting in the promise of freedom God gave them, they caved as Pharaoh pursued. They even said they wanted to return to Egypt and serve their harsh, cruel master. Sound like us in times of worry, in the presence of sin or that ex-spouse texting for a late-night "one for old times' sake"?

"As Pharaoh approached, the Israelites looked up, and there were the Egyptians, marching after them. They were terrified and cried out to the Lord. They said to Moses, 'Was it because there were no graves in Egypt that you brought us to the desert to die? What have you done to us by bringing us out of Egypt? Didn't we say to you in Egypt, 'Leave us alone; let us serve the Egyptians'? It would have been better for us to serve the Egyptians than to die in the desert!"
Exodus 14:10-12

It's initially understandable that you may not feel comfortable seeking Christian fellowship. Maybe it's because people feel they'll be judged by the church body. Nothing could be further from the truth if you are led to a bible-believing, Jesus-based body.

The old, Saturday Night Live "Church Lady" kind of church isn't the place that anyone can flourish and become healthy with the Lord. God's body of believers are the formerly broken and the currently under repair. Like you.

"That is, that I may be encouraged together with you while among you, each of us by the other's faith, both yours and mine."
Romans 1:12

Christians are the first to confess we're sinners and saved by God's grace. Many, if not all of us, have experienced the rough roads in life and have a soft heart for the brokenhearted. Christian fellowship is about service to others, not judgment over them.

"Therefore encourage one another and build up one another, just as you also are doing."
1 Thessalonians 5:11

9

SOUL TIES AND FORGIVENESS

"Casting all your anxieties on him, because he cares for you."
1 Peter 5:7

Forgiving yourself should seem like the simplest of all tasks for recovering from a nasty divorce. Unfortunately, our nature is to carry burdens to the cross, and then pick them up on our way back to the pew. Why can't we do as Christ instructed?

1 Peter 5:7 is pretty simple. Give all of your worries, anger, hate, fear, regret and perverted thoughts for revenge or evil-doing to God. He loves you and you are forgiven.

We know the reaction is to recoil at the thought of confessing to God that you have evil thoughts about the situation and/or your ex-spouse. Don't you think He already knows the condition of your heart? He wants you to understand that He knows, and for you to confess your heart so He can love you through those emotions.

God's not sitting up there waiting for your confessions with a rubber mallet like the kid's Whack-a-Mole game. Conversely, He's waiting to wrap His arms around you to help you dislodge the thoughts and emotions that separate you from receiving His will and incredible blessings.

Don't make the mistake I did by refusing to forgive myself and others during all of those years. I clung to the hurt like a badge of honor. Instead, it was a cancer that manifested itself in every aspect of my life. It was like a fog that settled over anything I did. Even the most incredible times of my life were immediately tempered by the haze of hate, fed by unconfessed sin.

Romans 8:1 is also proof positive that you are truly forgiven of your transgressions. This became important to understand later in my life when forgiveness became a stronghold that prevented pressing closer into Christ.

"Therefore, there is now no condemnation for those who are in Christ Jesus."
Romans 8:1

Your inability to forgive is based on the swing of emotion and not the everlasting Word of God almighty. You might, and probably should feel guilty or bad about the sinful things you've done. But feelings do not trump the sovereign word of Christ. Look at Romans 8:1 again —*"no condemnation."*

Ask God to help you forgive yourself, and even help free you from your past. You are a new creation in Christ. This also means God holds nothing against you. If He can put your sins awash, can't you? You can, if you truly seek and desire forgiveness—your own.

Forgive Others (including the Ex):

I know we covered forgiveness back in Chapter 6, but it's so critical to your recovery and positive forward progress with Christ that I wanted to share as it relates to others affected by divorce.

"Get rid of all bitterness, rage and anger, brawling and slander, along with every form of malice. Be kind and compassionate to one another, forgiving each other, just as in Christ God forgave you."
Ephesians 4:31-32

Why are we busying ourselves with forgiving others? First, it's commanded by God. Next, it's important to understand and anticipate that the ex-spouse isn't the only person who will hurt you during the divorce and recovery process. Don't be surprised when you're attacked once you've been blessed with a renewed and lasting relationship.

Looking at the entire sphere of those affected during the course of a divorce, you begin to see it's a much larger circle than only you and the ex-spouse. Some grievances continue to linger even after you and the former spouse reach a workable calm of civil avoidance.

While it's tempting to shrink that sphere and avoid those who may have offended you, it may be others as close as your own children that hurt you the most. They will need forgiveness from you as well as you benefiting from blessing them with sincere forgiveness.

God makes it crystal clear in Matthew 6:14-15 that if we forgive others, He will also forgive us, and that if we harbor unforgiveness toward others, that He will not forgive us.

Forgiveness is powerful, but it's a sword that cuts both ways. To forgive another person is a positive sign that you have reached a point in your post-divorce recovery where solid ground makes forgiving others possible.

Holding a grudge against someone because they wronged you entangles your spirit in a depressed condition. Do as Christ commands and become the liberator by casting the chains aside and experiencing the emancipation from harboring hurt against others.

We understand your carnal hesitation. It was you that was wronged after all, so why in the world should you forgive them? That is exactly the point—"in the world." You've got to "up" your understanding to a level of heavenly comprehension. Having the mind of Christ allows your vision to be that of a spiritual juggernaut.

Don't grow impatient with others. Forgiveness is an active process of maturing the spirit, and in no way means you approve of the offending behavior. While you will never condone the behavior, forgiving others allows you to release the negative feelings without negating your own.

A major benefit to releasing your spirit of the darkness associated with unforgiveness toward others is that the anger and resentment you carry is actually toxic, and subjects everyone, including your children to an unhealthy environment. Finally, taking the high road allows you to reaffirm that you've achieved solid footing.

"Bear with each other and forgive whatever grievances you may have against one another. Forgive as the Lord forgave you."
Colossians 3:13

Soul Ties

Next to learning about forgiveness, soul ties has had the most dramatic effect on my life. Honestly I had no idea what a soul tie was, but once I was taught and fully understood, it freed me completely.

Although the term soul tie is not found in the Bible, it is described throughout Scripture by terms such as two becoming one and souls stitched together for example. This is a supernatural bond between two people that transcends time or activity. Did you know that half of all divorced people still have feelings of love for their spouse as long as ten years after their divorce? Some never get over the feelings of hurt, hate, sexual longing and other emotional connections.

It's not because they are still in love with the ex-spouse, or that the rage of hatred continues to burn hot. The stitching of two souls once bound by marriage remains attached in the spiritual realm. Although your marriage didn't work out, it doesn't negate the holy covenant that involved both of you and God when you pledged your vows before Him. The reality is, marriage was designed to last forever, so those vows you made do not expire because some judge granted the divorce.

Let me put soul ties in this perspective so you will see the importance of breaking them when necessary. Soul ties between a married couple serve to keep the union strong and impenetrable from outside forces. When a spouse has an affair and soul ties are formed through physical and/or emotional tethers, they also become a force for attraction that pulls that person away from their spouse.

Soul ties are formed in various ways, but one of the most common is through sexual relations. Let's go to the very beginning and see what God says about the first married couple; Adam and Eve.

"That is why a man leaves his father and mother and is united to his wife, and they become one flesh."
Genesis 2:24 (NIV)

Not only was having sex an act of combining their lives, but sex also knitted their souls together. It's repeated in Ephesians 5:31 for emphasis. We want you to also read the reference in the New Testament's Mark 10:7-9 because it not only talks about the husband and wife, but anyone else who gets in the way.

7 "For this reason a man will leave his father and mother and be united to his wife, 8 and the two will become one flesh. 'So they are no longer two, but one flesh.9 Therefore what God has joined together, let no one separate."
Mark 10:7-9 (NIV)

God's not kidding around about connecting two people in a supernatural way. We try to justify adultery or lust in a million different ways, but it is offensive to God. Now, we said earlier that soul ties can also be between a spouse and another person. Check out this eternal truth from 1 Corinthians 6:16:

"Do you not know that he who unites himself with a prostitute is one with her in body? For it is said, 'The two will become one flesh.'"

If you had an affair, or if your ex-spouse did, it's important that besides seeking forgiveness, you also break the soul tie. They not only keep lovers connected, but become a transference portal for sin and negativity.

On the brighter side, soul ties connect friends deeper than office acquaintances or gym buds. Soul ties can create deep, spiritual bonds between friends such as the case between King David and Jonathan (1 Samuel 18:1.) These are the positive results of supernatural connections.

If you have connected in a positive way, then nurture it. If it's a negative force such as tethers to an ex-spouse or lover, then break then immediately.

This is how to severe soul ties and free yourself from a past of hurtful people, events or actions.

- Repent of all sins associated with what caused the soul tie. If you had an affair, then confess that to God (Hint: He already knows)
- Symbols, gifts or items representative of a person or event that created a soul tie should be returned, disposed of or destroyed. Rings, clothes, pictures and all of the "keepsakes" we stash away are very harmful. Rid yourself of idols.
- Confess and repent of any vows you might have made to that person or about an action. "I will never love again," or "No one will ever hurt me again," etc are forms of soul ties that connect you to something outside of God's will. Repent and free yourself.

- If you are holding anything against that person who created the soul tie, you must forgive—immediately!!
- Verbally renounce all soul ties in the name of Jesus. Some people even write them out and burn them as an act of symbolizing freedom from the pains of past ties.

We can't stress enough how vital it is to search yourself for the remnants of soul ties. They are not sweet memories that linger. They're supernatural restraints preventing you from moving forward and growing new, God-led relationships.

Search your shoe boxes, fire safes, way back in the closet and anywhere else where you stash "trinkets," rid yourself of these connectors. Their harm lies in your inability to part from them. Your freedom depends upon your willingness.

10

FOCUSING ON THE FUTURE

Leah and I fly all the time. Between us and the kids, we easily log over one hundred flights each year. On a Southwest Airlines hopper from Dallas to New Orleans during the pre-flight announcements I heard the steward say, "In the event of a change in cabin pressure, your oxygen masks will drop. If you are traveling with a child, place the mask on yourself first, and then the child. If you have more than one child with you, pick the one you like the most."

I laughed, but the reality of having to prioritize a decision if it were as critical as life or death weighed heavy. How many people would be able to focus on the task at hand? Could you?

Although divorce isn't life or death, it sure feels like it sometimes. The amazing news is, you're still among the living. We know this because you've made it this far in the book. Now it's time to focus. Focusing is probably still a challenge at this hazy period in your recovery, so it's equally important that we prioritize what to focus on.

I trust by this point you know that we're giving the truth to you straight. The truth is going to be shared with you even if it means you get mad at us. God brought us together through this book that He inspired, so the truth is what you'll get. Now with that in mind, I'm going to take a second to hop up here on my soapbox.

We hear people profess that their children are priority number one. Our first reaction is to ask that you make God your priority. He will provide for you and your kids. And taking a step back and as it might apply later on, after God, your spouse is destined to be your next priority. How does this apply to you now? Well, if your spouse wasn't your earthly priority, then that might've been a sign of impending trouble.

If in your future you meet someone and decide to remarry, please do not place your spouse behind your kids in priority. Your kids' new stepfather must hold the position of *numero dos* after God. If you just can't place your new spouse above your kids, then please do not continue in that relationship. It will fail. The spiritual chain of command will always be God, spouse, kids and everything else. Parenting is a temporary assignment, marriage is designed to last forever.

But, back to our current situation of what's important, then yes, if you're divorced then your children should be your focus. And yet we see social media posts of the parent out at the clubs, boozing it up, and looking like the kids are the last things on their minds.

This isn't to be judgmental or appear superior. We're here to tell you the truth. If the kids are your focus, then let them be your focus. On another note, when the time does come to meet someone that may just lead to a second chance at love, your collection of images of you holding your favorite beer bottles remain in cyberspace forever. Don't fool yourself into thinking possible suitors don't investigate your social media pages. What do you want them to see?

"But be doers of the word, and not hearers only, deceiving yourselves."
James 1:22

This brings us back to the point of this section—focus. You must identify all competing factors in your life. Don't sugarcoat it or ignore them. Trust us, the mortgage company cares nothing about your divorce.

Focus on You

The first item on your list has to be the same as the Southwest Airlines message. Take care of yourself first. I spent over twenty-five years preaching for officers to slow down and drive carefully while en route to an emergency call. You're no good to anyone if you don't make it to the scene, or become your own crisis because you crashed while barreling through red lights.

This is selfish time. This is also self-preservation time. You have to protect you before you will ever be able to protect anyone else. Even if you have no children involved in the situation, you still have to take care of you.

What does this look like?

It looks like everything we've discussed up to this point. Taking care of yourself focuses on seeking or growing an intimate relationship with God. In that relationship with Him, the fellowshipping with believers encourages you to ease out of your isolation shell. It also centers on you and your recovery so that both of your feet become firmly planted on solid ground.

> *"My feet stand on level ground; in the great congregation*
> *I will praise the LORD."*
> Psalm 26:12

Along with your Christian relationships, caring for you should also mean prioritizing your health, your career, education, and your finances to name a few basic but key concerns.

Focus on Others

Once you've established a solid foundation for yourself by dealing factually with what your life situation, then you're ready to extend yourself. This is the only way you're going to be able to completely focus on your children.

Guess what? Maybe they won't get to go to Disney this year or the next year or anytime soon. You cannot bribe children into processing their own emotions. Giving them everything on the internet for Christmas isn't going to bring the family back together either.

We know what kids need during this time more than anything. It's your love and attention they crave, and it's free. Yet in this world of instant gratification and one-click purchases, we feel compelled to buy our way out of the parental doghouse for causing little Johnny to cry.

The entire divorce situation stinks. It really does, but don't candy coat it for the kids either. Depending on their age and comprehension level, be very honest with them. It's the stability of love in turbulent times that we seek. Why wouldn't they?

Children have a sincere heart for God. Include them in church family and youth groups. They'll meet peers in similar situations which will do as much good for their recovery as your hugs and affirmation.

It's tough to consider focusing on others beyond yourself and kids, but service to others is important for learning to trust again. It might have been your ex-spouse's infidelity that destroyed your ability to trust anyone, or the hurt from losing a relationship with someone you trusted would be "till death do us part."

Becoming involved in something beyond yourself and your needs is a mighty way to ease into interpersonal relationships without heavy investments of emotion or vulnerability. Church families, small groups and outreach are the perfect avenue for reintegrating into the world of humanity.

Focus on Facts, Moderation, and Boundaries

This is also a time for focusing on the realities of your life as a divorcee. I know, that word hurts, and it really stinks, but it's what it is and until you're ready to accept that without the painful stain, you'll continue to meander in quasi-denial.

Your life has changed, and unless you walked out with a monster settlement, then the other 99.9% of us are required to see the facts as they are presented.

Do you have a job? Do you need a job? You wouldn't believe how many people are hyped into poverty while misleading themselves into believing there is a pot of gold somewhere in the community property settlement. Now is the time to focus on what you have to do to set the foundation for moving forward. There are blessings ahead waiting for a faithful you.

Moderation in all things is a key component at all times. While good health is important, how often have we witnessed drastic changes in appearance and other major life shifts with tragic results? Obsession, overdoing, and grasping at straws are results of feeling helpless.

I can attest that while cycling one-hundred-mile races through mountains and swimming across white-capped waters may have helped me get physically fit, it did nothing to feed my soul or help me become spiritually healthy. I would have better invested my time by combining activities with prayer and bible reading.

Remember, you are entering a new world that was very different before you and your ex-spouse met, dated, and married. Even in a brief relationship that ended in divorce, the other side of life changes rapidly. Proceed with caution, because not only is it unfamiliar territory, but you're also no longer the person you once were. Whether you feel it or realize it, you are still vulnerable.

It's also wise to set boundaries. Boundaries protect, not prevent. These are not meant to limit or restrict your recovery and relaunch, but to ensure you focus forward and remain clear about what you will and will not accept.

Right now, the most important boundaries you should set are in regards to your ex-spouse. If you have children involved, you must establish rules. Where will you exchange the kids, and will you allow the ex-spouse to come into your home or engage in joint activities for the "sake of the kids"?

It's not uncommon for ex-spouses to fall into a false calm for old times' sake. This usually results in regrettable sex and feelings of being used or more guilt. The best way to establish your solid single ground is to make your boundaries known to your ex-spouse so there are no hard feelings or unrealistic expectations.

Boundaries are meant for protection by keeping the lurking forces out of your property, your home and your life. Setting the ground rules now will minimize the control the ex-spouse has through texting demands, threats, or random nagging just to exert themselves back into your life. This can amplify once you've met and become interested in someone else.

Trust us, we've seen people divorced for many years, yet the second one of them is seen in public with someone new, the rampage of old emotions surfaces. Don't allow this to shake your foundation—make the rules, and make sure you both follow them.

Additional boundaries should include your dating practices. You've come to a point where looking out over a ledge means seeing the beauty of what lies beyond. It no longer symbolizes the potential for jumping off of it. Don't disrupt your tranquility with regrettable one-night stands or sex outside of marriage just because someone new takes notice. Be firm and articulate your boundaries.

Focus on Your Future

Let's walk through this journey and examine where you are or will soon be. You've found yourself divorced. No matter how or why it happened, it happened and a union you stood before God to vow would never end, has done just that—ended.

Because of the forfeiture through divorce, you've suffered and survived the various stages of loss and grief. Based on the foundation of knowing you'd get through them, you allowed the emotions to have their push and pull but never did you give up on who you were. You knew God had wonderful plans for you.

Whether you clung to the Rock of Christ, slipped and then scratched your way back to it in the midst of the storm, or discovered Christ for the first time in your life—you sought Him. Amen that you sought His will and desires for your life.

This brings us to where you are or will be—on solid single ground. You are on your way back up. Not just to level ground, but higher than you've ever known because of the promises of Jesus Christ. Continue to seek Him, read His word, pray to Him and fellowship with His beloved people. He will deliver on the sacred promises.

While there will continue to be tough times, prioritizing what items in your life require the most attention will whisk you away into the right stream of God's desire for your life. This is a challenging time because you're starting to regain confidence and can see the light at the end of what was once a very dark tunnel.

Is there new love at the end of that tunnel? That is between you and God, but whether it's a new relationship or a new puppy, it's an important time for you to remain focused on your recovery and sustainment through God's will and word.

11

CHALLENGES OF DATING

"Remember not the former things, nor consider the things of old. Behold, I
am doing a new thing; now it springs forth, do you not perceive it? I will
make a way in the wilderness and rivers in the desert."
Isaiah 43:18-19

Decisions to enter the dating arena are often made from self-assessments, peer pressure, or cultural expectations. The heart has healed and you feel led to expose yourself to the possibility of loving another. Hold tight as we share scripture and practical life lessons to help you navigate the challenges of starting a new romance.

Here's your first assignment. The next time you're on social media, we want you to look at the profile picture, the background cover or a few post feeds of friends, family or strangers. Really examine the content. It won't take long before you're reading their life's current situation. What do you see? Is it a picture of someone divorced, newly dating, playing the field or content to continue alone? Do you see yourself? Then avoid these situations at all costs.

While we all want to look our best for ourselves, each other or just because; this verse in 1 Peter below places "primping" and showboating into perspective. This new period of reentering the dating, single or divorced realm is vital to do the proper way. There's much more than scrubbing up and putting on your "fancy" clothes. Enter this phase as you've survived the tragedy of divorce—with grace by following God's plan. The apostle Peter warns us about putting on a public façade:

"Do not let your adorning be external—the braiding of hair and the putting on of gold jewelry, or the clothing you wear—but let your adorning be the hidden person of the heart with the imperishable beauty of a gentle and quiet spirit, which in God's sight is very precious."
1 Peter 3:3-4

Let your beauty be who you really are. Maybe your last experiences with dating were back in high school or college. Because years have passed and now you're back to dating doesn't mean you're back in that golden era. While there are still mean girls and meathead jocks out there, it doesn't require you to stoop for attention. Be beautiful in Christ and your light will shine.

Once you're cozy in single skin, and feel led to venture out among the unfamiliar world of dating, the pressure to prepare for dating takes over. The gym, community 5k races, girls' night out, guys' poker nights, new haircut and color, or the many get-yourself-ready-to-mingle cultural mores we burden ourselves with.

You'll have to deal with burdens and preparations, but it's not what dress to wear or whether to wear your baseball cap backward or to the side (hint: don't do either one.) Prepare spiritually for the possibility of meeting someone. Set your boundaries and expectations, and everything else will merge smoothly—relatively speaking of course.

"Desire without knowledge is not good, and whoever makes haste with his feet misses his way."
Proverbs 19:2

Are your desires to begin again based on sound Christian principles or simply a longing for companionship? Have you truly prepared yourself for an interpersonal collision with someone new? Let us ask you this one question before you begin: Are you willing to meet, mingle and accept a date invitation from a non-believer?

If 'your instinctual reply was, "I'm not sure, or it depends on the person I meet," then you are barreling down another path of destruction. Wanting companionship is understandable, but remember how the relationship went with your ex-spouse before the divorce?

Now back to our question about dating a non-believer. This is vitally important that you make this decision before walking out of the door for your first social reintroduction. It will be the most important dating decision you'll make right after you decide to start dating.

"Do not be unequally yoked with unbelievers. For what partnership has
righteousness with lawlessness? Or what fellowship has light with
darkness?"
2 Corinthians 6:14

We've discussed this with friends and found that there are about as many strong feelings as there are no feelings about this boundary. Restricting your eligible dating pool to believers only may seem like a risky move, but you're out for quality, not quantity, right?

The fact that they are a good person is irrelevant. We wouldn't expect you to date anyone who wasn't a good person. This is usually where our friends get less friendly and aimlessly decry, *"But they can change."* Everyone can change. What we hear when that bullet is fired our way is that they may not be as committed to starting anew or seeking a Godly relationship the next go around as they thought.

Can people change? Amen they can, and it's our responsibility to pray for unbelievers. But it is not wise to convert the kingdom of Christ one ex-spouse at a time. If you are honestly seeking a lifetime partner rather than a good-time gal or guy, then before the first hello, is the time to make a list of very firm decisions about what you want. Remember, boundaries are there to protect you.

This should be the easiest list you ever make—what you want should be what God has placed on your heart. I remember an old Burt Reynolds movie, *The End*, where he tried killing himself by drowning, only to change his mind. As he came closer to shore, the tone of his bargaining with God changed as did the conditions of his survival. While just a comedy movie, it illustrates how we react in the midst of crisis. Do you recall how sharp the pains were in the beginning stages of your marriage's destruction? Did you cry out to God? Did He deliver?

If you're actively reading this section about being strong enough to date, then amen, He did hear your pleas and delivered you—again. Don't be the Burt Reynolds' character who promised God everything while struggling, but nothing as he crawled ashore.

Make a list. Write it down. Share it with a close friend or spiritual accountability partner. When the winds of romance stir and you're happy someone takes notice of you, it's easy to tuck the list away. God graciously placed His desires in your heart. Do not ignore them. Of course, if you do, make sure you have a reserve of new friends willing to go through another break up, or at least old friends who promise not to taunt you with "I told you so."

I don't offer this advice without serious prayer and consideration. It took almost twenty years in the pit before God delivered Leah to me. The reason I didn't say "I waited," is because over those two decades, I made mistakes. But God first told me to be still, and each time I knew for sure that I'd met the next Mrs. Scott Silverii, God mercifully removed the crooked desire from my heart.

God spoke to me about a year before Leah came into my life, and I knew it would be time. I'd never prayed for a wife until that desire was placed on my heart. What I also learned later was that my pastor and his son had begun praying that God bring me a wife. Not only was God preparing Leah, but He was gathering the men I loved and would become my support team.

Was it worth the wait? Yes!!!

We'll move forward, but this simple decision will affect your potential for a lasting relationship based on biblical truths. Your heart may have healed from the hurt of divorce, but your mind should have been reprogrammed to be a bit more cautious.

Leah loves making lists, but I've tried to avoid including too many so far. I think things are changing. But in all honesty, this is the best way to share our information with you. These challenges to dating are important to consider, so please don't skip this list.

More Challenges to Dating

Other challenges associated with the potential for dating are that you may have the fear of getting burned again, which is often intermingled with self-doubt. Are you ready to meet someone new? Are you completely over your previous marriage and divorce?

Do you have the self-confidence to attract someone worthy of your decision to be vulnerable to an open heart? Are you really going to wear that shiny silver top on your date? Just kidding, but please make sure you're not so worried about getting burned that you allow the potential of meeting someone wonderful go up in flames.

Before we break out Leah's list of things to consider, one issue we've yet to mention is the obvious. The older you are, the more set in your ways you may be, and less willing to compromise or break habits non-conducive to a new relationship. I was fifty years old when Leah and I married and I'd been single almost 20 years. Do you think I had some deep-seeded, long-ingrained habits and no-go zones?

We've emphasized setting boundaries, and this one is as important as any other. This is your redo season. Do not settle for another version of your ex-spouse because the name is different. It's still a clone of your ex-spouse.

Even if you have to create a checklist of what you want in a partner and what you will not accept, then do it. We always encourage you to write out a prayer journal so you'll see God's answers to your prayers. Writing out your prayer qualities for a new partner should be part of your journal experience.

These are other areas with potential for challenging the positive dating scenario:

1. **Your baggage:** If you've been on this earth for more than a week, then you've accumulated baggage. Is it something you can leave behind or does it come with the new relationship? You must determine how to reveal it and how much of a role you'll be willing to have it play in the future.

2. **Their baggage:** You must, we repeat, you must define your terms for allowing someone into your life. We aren't talking about a second shot at the high school sweetie or the hottie down the block. If that's your mission, please stop reading this book, and go make the mockery of things that will occur. You must set boundaries, and part of that is what type of baggage and how much of it will you accept. Let's be honest, for example, not everyone is parent material. You don't have kids, do you now want kids? Do you want someone else's with the addition of an ex-spouse and parent to contend with?

3. **Parenting:** We love our kids, but there's nothing saying that a stranger might. Does the new person have children? Are they older and out of the home? Starting over with younger children can be as stressful as it is rewarding. Or do you or they want more kids, and are you willing to oblige? Kids are the single most important decision you'll make when deciding how to move forward. Move cautiously and choose wisely.

4. **Families:** Does their immediate or current family concern you? They may one day be your family as well. Conversely, is your family

on the FBI's most wanted list? Don't fool yourself into thinking extended family has no effect on a relationship, or that it'll be just the two of you against the world—this isn't junior high.

5. **Finances:** Can you really live on love? What's your new love's credit score? Are they a spender or a saver? Do they pay child support? Guess what? Their child support will be your child support. Do they have a retirement account? These are all questions you should know the answer to before you decide to walk down the aisle again.

6. **Relocation:** The world has expanded. Or at least our spheres of familiarity have. It's not uncommon to have long-term, meaningful relationships across the globe. Are you willing to relocate if necessary? How about uproot the kids from their school district and friends? Would you change jobs across country? If no, then stop the chitchatting and wish them well.

7. **Health:** Do you or your kids have special needs or particular health issues that would place a burden on the uninitiated? As a parent of a son with Down syndrome, I will attest that it was frightening when Leah and I first discussed our kids. It was because of God's love that she never batted an eye when I mentioned it or when she and her kids met him. They all love each other unconditionally.

8. **Career:** Have you worked hard to establish yourself in your field? Would you be willing to quit to be a stay-at-home parent? Are you a stay at home parent and you'd have to go back to work? Would they have to change careers, and what degree of strife will that cause to one or the both of you?

9. **Personalities:** They say opposites attract. That was cute for the jock and nerd. This isn't a 1980s sweetheart movie with Molly Ringwald. Often, the things you thought were cute and quirky become issues that annoy you unless it's understood that compatibility becomes possible through time and tolerance. Are you willing to struggle through to achieve harmony and spiritual oneness?

10. **Salvation:** This should be the most important issue. We've

covered it before, but it demands another call to attention. Are you willing to become involved with a nonbeliever? Remember your commitment to making your next marriage your last one. It's only by laying the relational foundation upon the Rock of Jesus Christ that you will live a blessed second chance.

We all have skeletons. Some even stay in the closet. Most don't. What and how much are you willing to share with your potential partner? When should you reveal your most sensitive issues, and if you do, what are the terms of their acceptability? We aren't trying to discourage you from finding happiness. But we do pray that joy is sought through God's desire as opposed to the warm and fuzzies of shallow acquaintances that threaten to repeat the course of your last failed relationship.

I thought it would be really funny to have Leah share her "dating" story with you. I'll just leave it at that, and let her explain.

Leah's Story

Hey there! It's me again. I've enjoyed reading the chapter on dating above. Scott gives some really good advice. You should listen to it. We can tell you by experience that it'll save a lot of heartache in your future.

What I mean by that is Scott and I did things the hard way. It's why you're getting this awesome book with so much great advice. We can tell you exactly what not to do because we likely did it in one fashion or another.

Like I said in a previous chapter, I was not ready to jump into a new relationship or get married when Scott and I started dating. I had a lot of healing to do. And despite the fact that Scott was single for twenty years before we married, he wasn't in a healthy place to get married or be in a serious relationship either. But we made the covenant, and we've stuck it out and worked through every speck of our lives so we could be healthy and whole. It's a lot easier to deal and heal with your own baggage than it is to deal with yours and someone else's at the same time. But like I said, we did things the hard way. And I wouldn't change it because our marriage has gone through the fire and is stronger for it.

I will give a word of caution to women who are entering the dating pool, and I know Scott goes into more detail in the next chapter. But women have to be very careful. I'd been married for twelve years before my divorce, and I'd never dated anyone except my ex-husband. I had zero experience in the dating arena.

What I did have at the time of my divorce was an established career and financial stability, which brings out a lot of single (and not so single) men who become interested in testing the waters. I also had four children at home and more responsibility than I could handle, but those who showed me interest weren't interested in that part of my life.

I once had a bestselling author tell me he thought we should have an affair because it would be interesting for our readers and increase both of our book sales. Now, I've never been accused of being a dummy, so I can only imagine what my facial expression looked like when he suggested this. I've been with exactly two men in my life, and my interest in affairs was zero. But I understood immediately that he had a use for me. Having an affair probably would've brought interest and book sales for him, because there's a different standard when it comes to men and sex, but it would've ruined me.

When I met Scott I was immediately pulled into his magnetic personality. We met at a writer's conference where he was teaching writers about SWAT and working under cover. I'm not going to lie, a man's brain is very attractive to me and when he started talking about his PhD in anthropology, all my little neurons started snapping. It didn't hurt that he has arms and shoulders like Hercules and a smile that can charm honey from the bees.

It also just so happened that one of my established series that I'd started writing years before had a hero who was exactly like Scott. I mean *exactly* like Scott. From his background in SWAT to his advanced education to his position as chief of police to the same tattoo that SWAT cops have. It was...interesting.

Scott's also a really good teacher and an engaging lecturer. By the time that class was over I had pages of notes, new story ideas, and a whole lot of questions. I'd mostly forgotten about his Herculean arms and bee charmer's smile. Mostly.

So I walked up to him after class with my head full of ideas and questions and told him he was exactly like one of my characters. Scott likes to tell people this was my pickup line. For those of you who've read my story, you know I have zero dating experience and no game, so the possibility of me using a line like this on a man like Scott was somewhere between no way and never.

But he did invite me to come visit his agency and do some more in depth research. I didn't realize until I got there how neatly he'd reeled me in. The rest, as they say, is history.

12

CAUTION: DATING AHEAD

Until retirement, I'd been a cop my entire adult life. We don't trust anyone. It's not a bad thing. It just means we question everything until proven true or false. It's a shame, but we cannot completely trust most people at face value. I've a saying that I apply to work and personal life: "Trust, but confirm."

While I've experienced it in law enforcement, it's also true in most people's daily interactions with others. Maybe they don't rise to the level of a life-sentence murder confession, but little slip-ups between newly met couples soon add up to something equally suspicious.

Being cynical is something I'm sure you have become since the rub of your divorce. It can be considered a gift as long as it's applied in the right setting. Of course, calling every potential suitor a liar isn't the best practice either. Just be aware of cynicism as you move forward in a potential relationship. You've gained a sixth sense since your divorce experience. Trust it.

Now this is the cop talking in me when I caution you about interacting with others. It's because I've spent my entire life protecting others, and although retired, it doesn't mean I can put my concern on hold.

You must remain somewhere between cautious and suspicious while you get to know someone. The trick is keeping it close to your vest without insulting your date. Always try to answer this one question by asking the right things and tucking away responses for consistencies or circle-back-facts:

What is their motivation?

Without coming across as a hard-nosed detective, you can uncover their motivations by mentally filing away facts they claim, stories they share, outcomes of past relationships they confide and anything else they offer to reel you in. Even if you have to type or text notes to yourself about names, dates, locations, jobs, etc. that they share; do it.

It is your responsibility to keep track of whether they remain consistent with details in other meetings, texts and conversations. In addition to your new sixth sense, God gave you a supernatural spirit of discernment. Use it to filter possible threats to a positive experience or truth stretching to impress you. Because defending yourself and eventually your kids if this meeting turns into a real relationship is so important, we reference two warnings from God:

"But examine everything carefully; hold fast to that which is good; abstain from every form of evil."
1 Thessalonians 5:21-22

and,

"Do not believe every spirit, but test the spirits to see whether they are from God; because many false prophets have gone out into the world."
1 John 4:1

Leah and I have a close friend who'd gone through a traumatic divorce. I think I've taken on a role of protective big brother because each time we see her I make sure to ask about her dating life. Actually, I always tell her not to date a cop because they'll make a mess of her life. Of course, I'm kidding...kind of.

Anyway, she shared the story of meeting a nice man with whom she was interested in pursuing a relationship. Problem was, one red flag after another presented itself. I mean, like, really big, glaring red flags with warning horns blaring at her. But as people do, she either explained it away without asking because she didn't want to offend him, or when she mentioned something, he had an alibi or an accusation to throw back at her.

I sat in horror listening to the details of this guy's misgivings. Names that didn't match on prescription bottles left in his car, an email address of the name on the pill bottle that he said wasn't his, switching license plates on his car, not allowing her to visit his home, and so on and so on.

The only reason I knew she hadn't been kidnapped and killed was because she was standing in front of me. I begged her to drop him.

Months later we ran into her again. Guess what? She'd kind of halfway taken my advice, but mister inconsistent continued to work himself back into her life until she finally hired a private investigator. I'm sure you've figured it out by now that he was a career criminal and sex offender who was avoiding law enforcement because he'd failed to register in his new location as required by law. Our dear, sweet friend also has several very young children.

As I write this, I cannot tell you for certain she has completely cut ties with this mystery man. But I can tell you that there are an unlimited number of people whose personal stories just don't add up. It's your life, and no one should have to work harder at making it right than you. Don't be fooled by a sweet smile or a sad story.

I don't want you to walk away from this section swearing off people because of paranoia, but please be aware that while not everyone is out to get you, not everyone is sincerely praying to meet a nice single parent with the history of divorce.

These four are the most dangerous and common types of victimization experienced by the newly mingling divorcee. Please be on the lookout for people who are seeking:

1. **Sex:** Victimizers target divorcees because they have a skewed idea that you'll be appreciative of their attention, or since you've been without sex for a while, that you must be eager to have it.

2. **Money:** Child support and community property settlements can be seen as easy targets. Many recently divorced people make big changes in appearance or buy new cars, homes, vacations as a way to cope with the season of turmoil. These expenditures can be seen as having become wealthy, and it makes you an attractive target.

3. **Babysitter/kid raiser:** Single parenthood isn't easy. Playing the numbers game, it's always easier for two adults to manage kids than one. Beware of the single parent looking only for a partner in parenting. Our human compassion is on high alert when on the subject of single parents. A natural desire to help can become a hook for this type of victimizer.

4. **Ulterior or perverted intentions:** I hate to go here, but I'd be remiss if there wasn't a dire warning to trust your instincts, your family and those who sincerely care about you and your kids. Child abusers prey on divorced parents for the easy access to their true targets. Just writing this section breaks my heart for the heinous things I've experienced as a law enforcement professional. Most crimes may have been prevented by having given and following this simple advice.

Again, we're here to encourage you, but ultimately your safety is more important than your dating life. These items are important, and worth keeping in mind as you pursue the potential for a new relationship.

I'll jump ahead of Leah's testimony to tell you that we had our issues before moving forward. For me, I was, and still am fifteen years older than her. It was an issue I had to work through as it chipped away at my self-confidence. Prayer settled that one for me.

Finances, geography, and careers were but a few of the major challenges we faced long before either said, "Okay" or "I will" or "I do." Like I said, I'll leave the rest up to her to explain, you know, just in case she decides to share "too much."

Leah's Story

Like I mentioned before, we did things the hard way. If you've never taken Les and Leslie Parrott's SYMBIS (Saving Your Marriage Before it Starts) test, then I encourage you to do so if you're considering getting remarried.

Scott and I didn't know about the test then, we were both Christians but we didn't have a relationship with the Holy Spirit, we were filled with sin, pain, unforgiveness and secrets.

Our age difference was a minor issue. It bothered Scott a lot, and I have never, even to this day, looked at him and thought of him as fifteen years older than me. It doesn't bother me one bit. But it was an issue that gave him pause in whether or not we were going to move forward.

Our finances were another issue. Like I said in the last chapter, I was financially independent, and he was a chief of police. The financial disparity bothered him. I never thought anything of it. But we had a big issue when Scott suggested he sign a pre-nup. I was angry and insulted at the suggestion. Because the second I heard pre-nup, I thought, *he's already looking for an out-clause.*

We also lived in different states, had demanding careers where we both had to travel a lot, had seven children between us, two different child support arrangements, alimony, exes, future in-laws that weren't exactly hospitable, relatives looking for a free handout, and secrets. Lots of secrets.

Scott had been a cop for twenty-six years and had spent twelve of that working a double life undercover. This did not translate well into marriage. There were things he told me right before we got married he should have told me early on. I found out after we got married that he'd been engaged not long before he met me. And there were things I found out even later into our marriage that were devastating to me and could've ended our marriage.

My point is, ask questions. If someone asks you to marry them or if your relationship becomes more serious, it's your right to ask what you need to ask and get straight answers. If they get defensive, or offended, or act like it's none of your business, take a step back and slow things down. Because it'll be your business the second you say, "I Do," and by then it's too late. You get what you get, and any problems are yours whether you want them or not.

13

GETTING SERIOUS

"And I will give you a new heart, and a new spirit I will put within you. And I will remove the heart of stone from your flesh and give you a heart of flesh."

Ezekiel 36:26

The euphoria of a new romance can be exhilarating. It's a new start, a new chance, and a renewed lease on life. Making empowered decisions, and having the full knowledge that you're accepting the partner God intended is the singularly most positive aspect of this season.

Dating isn't addressed in the bible. It wasn't a cultural custom used for two people to try on the outfit of marriage. The bible specifically outlines three types of relationships between men and women— platonic friendship, brother/sister in Christ, and marriage. While not addressed in relation to marriage, the first two types of relationships aren't necessarily a bad idea for progressing towards marriage.

Courtship is a relatively new phenomenon. Maybe that's why we've yet to understand or perfect it. While this process isn't mentioned biblically, it doesn't mean there aren't principles guiding appropriate behavior. These are your decisions to pray over, but we want to remind you that making the same decisions as before will result in the very same outcomes.

Pray before you even entertain the notion of dating. Allow God to place His desire for dating in your heart. This is serious business when you consider what you've just gone through. Is it really something you want to rush into to spare a few lonely Friday nights? But, once you hear God's charge to charge, then charge with caution and optimism.

This is the redo. For whatever the reasons you initially became enmeshed in a relationship that led to your first marriage, there were fundamental flaws—hence the divorce. This is your chance to slow the spin, leverage hindsight to your advantage, and make rational choices.

It's hard to do that as a nineteen-year-old when birds are tweeting around your head and hearts throb in your eyes. Not to be a buzzkill, but this isn't stars and roses time. You've already once overlooked all the obvious signs that pointed to failure like a flashing highway sign in the midnight rain. Be the mature person who just endured one of the worst storms in their life.

We've made a list (yes, Leah was back at it) of the positives associated with a new beginning. While it may not have cosmic consequences, they are a dose of Christian common sense questions and opportunities that abound once you've set your wants in line with God's will.

1. **Realign Priorities:** Making a list of what you want and what you refuse to settle for in this new opportunity will help you articulate the primary focus of the relationship is Jesus Christ. It's understandable that while married at a younger age you may have been more focused on your education, career, travel, friends, extended family, hobbies, old high school and college friends, spouse or young kids. This time,

keep it simple and improve your chances for lasting success—place God directly in the center of your relationship.

2. Fresh Start: How many Mondays have we promised to begin the diet and failed, or Saturday blockbuster house cleanings that went untouched, or gym memberships that expired after only a few visits? I admit that the difference between being able to sustain a 21-day fast and not being able to diet until lunch is that my cause was greater than my circumstance. This is truly your time to shine, but first you have to know exactly what it is that you will and won't be polishing. Fresh starts are fun, unless they're actually repeats of past poor performance.

3. Chance to Do It Better: When considering the trauma you'd just survived, and that God set your feet back on solid ground, it really is a blessed opportunity to do it better. While maybe the divorce wasn't your fault, it is still your second chance at pulling close to Christ and asking for guidance in every aspect of your life. If a new relationship is within God's will for you, this is also the time to self-assess and identify areas where you can improve and bring your A-game into a new relationship. Many people we speak with share that they were never able to talk with their spouse, and never prayed together. This should be a priority in determining whether you'll consider dating nonbelievers.

4. Renewed Lease on Life: Next to grieving the death of a loved one, divorce has to rate up there as far as raw misery goes. It definitely has one of the most detrimental effects on a person. The potential for happiness and true joy are boundless when entering into the promises of a successful relationship. We tend to tote our failures, regrets and sins around like the two giant luggage trunks Tom Hanks carried in *Joe Versus the Volcano*. God forgave us, so you forgive yourself. Leave the luggage at the door, and allow yourself the chance to gain a new, vibrant perspective on life, love and marriage.

5. Not Having to Settle: Why did you get married the first time? Hearts and butterflies, pregnancy, peer pressure, all your friends did it, bored, to escape the family home? There are a crazy number of reasons why you married the first time. There's usually one reason it failed. Because the only foundation the marriage was based on was the first reason. Guess what? You've now had the benefit of life and time and experiences, both good and bad. You do not have to make those same decisions again. You do not have to settle. God has a glorious plan for you. Refuse to settle.

How Will You Know?

This is a great question. We've heard the old standby, "You just know." If by that you mean God confirmed your prayer petitions to show you the right path, then okay. But at this point in life, trusting your gut or your heart or your best friend shouldn't be a consideration.

If you are going to trust God on this one, then there is no give and take. You've got to practice patience no matter how hard your heart flutters or the new love is pressing you for a commitment. Time is your friend, and in God's timing should be your only plan.

> *"Every word of God proves true; he is a shield to those who take refuge in him."*
> *Proverbs 30:5*

Opening yourself up to becoming sensitive in detecting God in others is a wonderful blessing. It's a spiritual radar detector. Learn to trust it. It's seldom wrong. If your early warning system is pinging at the presence of someone you're interested in, please don't walk away. Run.

Time will tell once you've allowed the emotional churn to settle. Draw close to God through prayer. Even closer than you've ever been, and ask Him to guide you in the relationship. You've prayed for a second chance, so don't accept second best.

Leah and I want only the best for you, so please don't accept what we share as taking anything lightly. This is serious business and we've both been on the receiving ends of troubled times. We've said it before, but had there been this type of book available during our respective storms, maybe we'd come through without as many scars.

I know personally the years of wondering and worrying about why I felt the way I did caused horrible stress. Making the matter worse was that I had been saved in a Christian church, and was supposed to have known better. During those years there were good people set in my path. I trusted they wanted to help, but at best their advice left me unfulfilled and questions unanswered.

Yelling, "Swim," to a drowning person isn't going to save them, but tossing a floatation ring or reaching out a hand will. Leah and I are grateful God laid this topic on our hearts. I've made so many messes since my first divorce, that writing this resource still turns over painful soil. Practical advice and real-life examples would have been so much more helpful at that time. We truly pray this is your helping hand.

14

BEFORE YOU SAY "I DO"

You're ready, you're willing and you're able to move forward with a new, loving relationship. You've considered everything listed in the chapters above and more. It's going to be amazing and God is set squarely in the middle of your efforts.

Amazing that is except for this one little interruption. It's like the old junior high school activities where chaperones flooded the slow-song dances to warn you both to, "Make room for Jesus."

Yes, let's take a small step back and consider a few more challenges you may have faced, are facing, or will face as this new relationship continues to blossom. We know it sounds like a lot to hassle with. After all, love is supposed to be pure and simple, and magical, right?

While love is the greatest, it's not love that complicates relationships in a real-world environment. People do. Sin does, and proceeding without a plan will. I know we're dumping lots of things to consider in this and the last few chapters, but we've been there. And to be honest, we were there not too long ago, so this is still fresh on our hearts. There's a reason second and third marriages fail much more than first marriages do. These are some of the major issues, so we'd be doing you no favors by ignoring them.

"So now faith, hope, and love abide, these three; but the greatest of these is love."
1 Corinthians 13:13

Complex Family Tree

To quote those agitating television high-pressure salespeople, "But there's more." It's difficult enough to find the perfect mate, but with God, there's hope. Remember, He promised all things are possible, not all things are easy.

The biggest, reddest hot button for any couple are kids. Married, biological parents cite conflicts over their very own kids as one of the greatest sources of strife in their marriage. Let's look at two unmarried people with their own children from another adult relationship, who will attempt to not only consensually combine their lives, but enmesh the lives of their respective children as well. That was a mouthful.

Leah and I were attending a FamilyLife Weekend to Remember[1] marriage conference in San Antonio, Texas. They played a short animated video about the realities of blending a family. It blew our minds to see a visual representation of the complexities in blending.

Oftentimes, we focus on the man and woman. We discuss the kids and what's best for them, but despite what they say, we'll make sure they like it. Done and done. Everyone is happy in this nice, tight circle—right?

Assuming you've remarried, what about your new spouse's kids, parents, siblings, extended family, work associates, social circles, their ex-spouse, their ex-spouse's in-laws, ex-spouse's extended family, your new spouse and their ex-spouse's mutual friends, co-workers, mutual social and professional associations?

How about your ex-spouse? The kids you share, your ex-spouse's parents, siblings, extended families, mutual friends shared by you and your ex-spouse, your ex-spouse's new spouse, the new spouse's kids, parents, siblings, extended family, friends, mutual circles of associates, etc.

Can you see where this is heading? We've all been there, done that and got the divorce decree to prove it. The next and last time around has to be thoughtfully considered. The failure rate of second and third marriages prove it. If you think love will conquer all and the kids, kinfolk and K-9s will enjoin in harmony, you're kidding yourself.

Reduce the Risks

Let's not leave this relationship to chance. Protect your marriage and the blended family with facts and the reality of challenges you both face going into this relationship. We will attest that there were many issues once we began discussing the reality of marriage. While some rocked us back on our heels, none knocked us to the floor. God has gotten you this far. He will not abandon you.

"It is the Lord who goes before you. He will be with you; he will not leave you or forsake you. Do not fear or be dismayed."
Deuteronomy 31:8

We created a hot sheet of challenging topics recommend for you both to give earnest, God-centered consideration to. We want you to see this again where we said, "you both." If your new love is not open to discussing now, do not expect them to be open to the idea once locked in. Failure to discuss this is a deal breaker.

You don't have to agree on everything, but the key is to begin engaging in open dialogue about more than sugar kisses and sweet cheeks. Some topics are open for negotiations while others are not.

We had a friend recently who reached out to ask what we thought about her fiancé's insistence that after they were married each would keep their own monies in separate accounts. He suggested she pay the bills, mortgage and expenses and then invoice him for his half, and he'd pay her within ten days.

Oh, and she said he let her know it was not up for discussion just in case the marriage didn't work out.

What would've been your advice to her? What suggestions do you think we offered? Now, are there instances where this scenario would work in a solid marriage? Sure there are. But are they biblically based? No, not at all according to God's foundational law of marriage concerning possession. Pastor Jimmy Evans teaches from Genesis 2:24 that when the two shall become one, that everything is rolled up into one. No longer man or woman, but marriage.

"That is why a man leaves his father and mother and is united to his wife, and they become one flesh."
Genesis 2:24

These are the items we highlight and you must decide what you are and aren't willing to compromise.

The following list of hot topics are in order of the most often discussed, debated and fought over. These have either led to divorce or stopped marriages from happening in the first place.

Friends, this is not another one of those tough love zones. If you are too uncomfortable or dread opening up the conversation with your partner, then maybe it's not time to move forward. This is also a perfect litmus test for determining suitability as marriage material.

More of Leah's Lists

1. **Children:** We'd like to think this would be all that needed to be said, but unfortunately, it's the least discussed topic between couples. We don't mean that couples don't talk about their kids, but posting

social media pics and boasting about grades isn't the conversation we're referring to. There has to be genuine conversation about bringing existing children into your new love environment.

Remember, they're not the ones who've met mister or missus wonderful. On the flip side of the relationship coin are your partner's children and their reaction to you. There is so much at stake, let's not rush into this. Did you catch that we said existing children? Future children through either conception and birth or adoption is also a super-hot topic we pray you'll have with each other.

2. Finances: This is usually when we hear crickets. Two independent adults have struggled to survive not only the emotional and psychological trauma of divorce, but the financial damages as well. One or both of you may still be entangled in debt and or continuing support (child/spousal) payments.

Add to this topic the previous challenge of kids, and money becomes even more entwined in complexity. We like the phrase, "Is your money married or just dating?" All in is all in. While some couples successfully maintain separate accounts, most fail as it leads to suspicion and in-fighting. We're big fans of the Dave Ramsey series on finances. We highly recommend it.

3. Careers: This is usually associated more with identity than finances. People work hard to succeed in their chosen professions. Will you give up yours for the sake of the family unit? Are you willing to become the stay-at-home parent or subject yourself to the bread-winner's rule?

We become very entrenched in what we do. It sometimes defines who we are. This topic doesn't fall far behind finances on the list. Let's go the opposite direction. What if you've been the stay-at-home parent for all of your children? Are you willing to abandon the kids at daycare to reenter the workforce? Have you and your partner discussed this?

Do you see where kids and finances tie into this and are ranked numbers one and two? It's all combined, and deserve equal attention prior to taking the next step in life. Failure to address these issues is guaranteeing another failed marriage.

4. Geography: In eras as recent as the 1950's and '60's, most people married the person literally next door. At most, typical long-distance relationships expanded just a few city blocks. People often grew up, married and raised their families within the same neighborhoods and towns.

Modernization of the transportation system saw more than interstate commerce boom. So did the stretch of geography for people meeting their eventual partners. Take it a step more virtual, and the internet connected the globe to a possibility of zero boundaries between lovers. Do you both live in the same town, are all of the kids in the same region, or where has either of your jobs called for you to relocate?

People think it's tough leaving home for college? Try living in one place for decades with an established network of family and friends, and then uprooting to follow the partner of your dreams into unfamiliar terra firma. You want to talk about stress? You must discuss geography.

5. Home: Whose home will we make our new home? That's simple right? Your home. Wait a second, maybe it's not so simple. Maybe your partner wants to remain in the home where their kids were raised and they return each holiday to continue family traditions.

Would it make you uneasy to move into the home your partner and their ex-spouse built together? How about sleeping in the same bed they once made love in? Not feeling so cozy after all, are you? It's natural. What's not natural is for two people who have already been burned by life's nastiness to fail to avoid the same pitfalls that led to prior divorce.

Talk about home sites before you shove your toothbrush in the vacant holder. Maybe you both can't afford to buy a neutral new location to start fresh in, and in that case, be super considerate of the other person's sensitivity towards occupying once used space. Home is where the heart is after all.

6. Toxic ex-spouse: Guys are notorious for not being open about the potential for conflict between a new partner and an ex-spouse. Even a Glenn Close-type character from *Fatal Attraction* is minimized as just a jealous, jilted former lover. Consider the reality of your ex-spouse's potential for volatility and conflict. Are they prone to violence, calling the police or stalking?

Your new love deserves to know the landmines before tipping a toe into the tainted fields. If you have children involved and custody / visitation court decrees, your new partner becomes as much a part of the turmoil as you are. Be open and honest about your relationship assessment with your ex-spouse. This isn't to say all ex-spouses are troublemakers, but toxic ones are direct threats to the success of your new marriage. Don't blow it off as being dramatic.

7. Identity: While you were married, your identity should've been entrenched with that of your spouse. Once you divorced, you probably had a harder time establishing your own identity than the one of a unified couple when married. It's because once newly single, you've not quite figured out who you are on your own.

One question that always bothered me was on forms that asked divorced or single. It had been almost 20 years, so I figured I'd deserved the ability to just be plain single. The fact was, I was and always will be a divorcee. It's like an ink stain on your shirt. You can flap your tie or coat over it, but the stain is always going to be there, even if it's only you who sees it. Now, what becomes as important as how you see yourself now, is how you will identify yourself when you meet someone new.

Since you'd been through an identification retooling post-divorce, will you be as willing to join identities with someone new? I know we referenced this verse earlier, but it's so crucial to a God-covenant marriage, that we'll share it again. It's not a matter of giving up who you are, but the process described in Genesis 2:24 of becoming one with your partner.

"Therefore a man shall leave his father and his mother and hold fast to his wife, and they shall become one flesh."
Genesis 2:24

Bad Habits

Along with your willingness to combine identities into a seamless union is recognizing you have established habits in your past life; both previously married and single/divorced. You must also understand that your new love has also picked up habits along the way. Are you willing to compromise and accept? It's always easier to say than to actually do.

We've heard people surprised that their partner didn't follow through on changing behaviors or habits such as smoking or limiting shopping and spending money without regard for a multi-person household. Habits are hard to break, so talk about them before falling into another trap of falsely believing you can change the person.

We understand this seems like a contradiction between God will deliver you the mate He has for you, and a few warnings about being watchful for areas of conflict and compromise.

Some might even conceive that if God delivered the partner, then the partner would arrive pristine and without smelly shoes and no stalker ex-spouse peering through windows. There's a stark contrast between praying for God to introduce you to your next spouse, and making out a child's Christmas wish list.

We are adults, and we come as fractured as we come marvelous. You must be responsible enough to avoid past trappings. Do not marry the same person, with just a different name. Have these conversations early and often. Is this a chance to start fresh—yes. Is it a reality that by avoiding necessary conversations about sensitive topics that your fresh start may result in a similar stale conclusion—most definitely.

Seek the wonderful opportunities, and smooth the potential pitfalls. God has something wonderful for you, and it might be in the form of a blessed new start.

"For I know the plans I have for you," declares the Lord, "plans to prosper you and not to harm you, plans to give you hope and a future."
Jeremiah 29:11

15

MARRIAGE: GOD'S DESIGN

We pulled it off. Not a single one of our invited family had a clue that the supper they'd come to was actually our surprise wedding. It went off without a hitch and we were so happy that it went down the way it did. Between both of our very public profiles, there was way too much expectation for our wedding, so we kept it quiet. Very quiet. We wanted the focus on Christ, not guest lists.

Even our kids, who were surprised, enjoyed it. We were relieved. Our pastor, who obviously was in on the plan, came to say good-bye as the evening began to wrap up. Excited, he asked where we were off to for our honeymoon. We kinda shrugged while looking back at our five small kids and Leah's mom, who also lived with us.

"Well, we're packing up the Suburban and heading back home. We've got lots of work to do," I confessed.

The next week after church, the pastor pulled us aside and explained that marriage is to be celebrated. We knew that, but it took an honest reminder to enforce it. We immediately remedied it with a four-day bicycle tour of Northern California's wine country.

Unfortunately, Leah isn't a cyclist and long miles on a skinny seat don't make for much romance after a day's trek. She scheduled the trip because of my love of cycling. See, those are the small sacrifices spouses make for each other. Of course, I've gone along on lots of shopping trips too.

So outside of a surprise wedding, a stern reminder from the pastor and a bike tour, what are the keys to this mystery called remarriage? Let's take a look at God's intended purpose for marriage, how remarriage differs from your first attempt, and divorce-proofing this one so it thrives and lasts the way God designed it to.

Remember; For marriage to be important, you must treat the marriage as important.

God's Design

I've tried to bite my tongue as pseudo-intellectuals espouse that the essence of man was no more important than the beasts, birds and fish. They've claimed God made us sexual creatures only to procreate and fill His world with lots of little people who resembled Him.

Now, before we smash that softball out of the park, I'd like to ask you what do you truly feel was the purpose of God creating us? Was it to populate the earth? Or maybe it was to tend to His animals like hired hands? Do you trust that God created man and woman in His image because He loved us? Do you also believe that God created marriage to reflect the relationship He wants to have with us?

Oh, and to get back to the previous paragraph, I don't engage in arguments over what I know the truth to be. God is the truth, and it's all I share, and yes, we are meant to be more than beasts. So now that we're on the same page, let's have the "M" talk.

God didn't create us because He was lonely, He had perfect company with His Son and the Holy Spirit. Together, they created man.

"Let us make man in our own image."
Genesis 1:26

God created us because He loved us even before we were conceived.

"I have loved you with an everlasting love."
Jeremiah 31:3

To further the loving relationship, God created marriage. Throughout the Old and New Testaments, God references the relationship with He or His Son as the groom and the church, His people as the bride.

That's pretty simple. You are carrying on in the tradition of marriage designed to grow the relationship God wants to have with us. You and your spouse are the image bearers of God's design for relationships. How's that for putting you under pressure?

We know you can handle it. Look how far you've come from those early, dark days. To give you an even more specific idea of why God designed marriage, there are a few practical applications for it.

1. **Partnership:** After God created Adam, He was pleased with man. I'm guessing Adam was a pretty good guy. But God quickly saw man was not meant to be alone. He needed a helper. Eve was created to be his wife, and God was again pleased because man did indeed need a partner.

2. **Deeper Intimacy with God:** Man on his own is going to remain being a man. This usually continues until his demise at his own doing. That's kind of a joke, except that Leah isn't laughing. Men need Godly women who respect gender roles and the special gifts God has graced them with to help them soften the hardness most men are predisposed to carry around like a gold medal.

Likewise, women can grow deeper in faith and stronger in their walk with God with the strong, spiritual guidance of a spirit-filled husband. We've discussed the original definition of woman as helper, and that in no way was it intended to imply less than man. Through God's hierarchy, women thrive in the marriage model.

3. Pursue God Together: Have you ever heard two heads are better than one? 'Well, in this case, two hearts are better than one, or none. God made it very clear that man needed woman. Not to lord over her, but as his helper to do great things through great strength and gifts. God created marriage to mirror His relationship with us, so it would only make sense that together as man and woman, pursuing God is more natural and in line with what God ordained at the very beginning with Adam and Eve.

Actually, going back to the beginning is a great idea. Gaining an understanding for the very first marriage is vital for a deeper appreciation of the marriage covenant. Unless you know the origin of marriage, you'll likely repeat 'its failure.

The very first marriage covenant was between God, Adam and Eve. God created marriage as a reflection of the intimate relationship He wants to share with us. The first couple were designed to be the image bearers of God's love. Is it any wonder why satan moved in on the newlyweds so immediately?

Satan saw the depth of intimacy between man and woman and more importantly, with God. While he held no authority over man and woman, he did exercise influence. What better way to attack God than to wound His most beloved? Temptation was crafted to wedge the separation within God's covenant.

Satan held no power over God, but before man and woman were created in God's image, there was nothing between the devil and God. While Adam and Eve's actions may have shifted the boundaries of the marriage relationship, it never diminished the love of God for His people.

The creation of the first marriage also changed the dynamic from a sovereign God who loved to create, to a nurturing God who yearned to love His creations.

Covenant

The marriage covenant is God's holy oath between your spouse, you and Him. It is unbreakable, non-negotiable and irrevocable. Once we begin to take this seriously, we will become serious about getting started for a real, lasting covenant commitment. This is a fresh start and a rare redo in life. You know new love because God gifted you with true love. Marriage is sacred. It is His bond because it is His word. His word is truth.

> *"Sanctify them in the truth; your word is truth."*
> *John 17:17*

Society on the other hand, has watered down the dynamics of marriage by interchanging the terms of a Bible-based union from covenant to contract. The differences are critical and allow for the weakened degree of consensual agreement to better fit today's liberal agenda.

Divorce is accomplished much easier when thought of in terms of a civil contract. Gay marriage is justified as a lawful marriage because it's considered nothing more than a civil contract. Thinking in terms of the temporal contract opens the door for marriage variations never intended by God.

The problem with a civil contract is that they are intended to benefit each individual entered into the agreement. This doesn't require selflessness or giving to the other party. It is completely a matter of what do I get out of this contract. The contract is also negotiable even as proposed, entered into and throughout the life of the deal. Shifting of values, priorities and commitments are inconsistent with the stability of a God-centered marriage.

A contract is enforceable by man's law, and often with the threat or intimidation of tangible consequences. Inaction, absence of choice or unwillingness to participate carries civil and legal penalties. The covenant is not forced but is a choice willingly entered into out of selfless love and personal commitment.

One of the biggest differences between the two is that a contract usually requires a fifty-fifty benefit for each party. Marriages with spouses who only give half, always end up with nothing. The covenant desires to offer each other one hundred percent of everything they are, have and will be. Finally, contracts come with expiration dates.

Covenants last forever. So can your marriage.

16

FIRST TO FINAL MARRIAGE

Different From the First

The rational person might think that a second marriage would be so much better than the first because there'd be no way of making the same mistakes that led to the failure the first time. It's all about experience.

Experience is what we base job applications on, salaries are usually weighed against the experience an applicant brings to the table, sporting events are usually predicted based on the level of experience as a team or skilled player position. So by all accounts, you've got experience at being married and the next time will thrive thanks to it.

Okay, what about bad experience? Years on a job do not mean the employee was productive at that job. It might mean they learned to manipulate the system to get by. What if a quarterback has thrown twenty passes with one touchdown and nineteen interceptions? What if you're getting married a second time because of the horrible experience from the first time?

Let's not settle into a cozy cocoon called experience. The truth is, most remarried people carry the same baggage and make the same mistakes that damaged their first marriage. Another kick in the pants is that people often marry the "same" spouse but with a different name. There are human characteristics we are drawn to; for good or bad. Let's not set ourselves up for failure once the flames of passion simmer because we relied on experience.

Another thing to consider is that avoiding past mistakes in a former marriage is not a solid foundation for basing your new relationship. If all you do is work to avoid the bad stuff from before, you will never experience the great stuff in the present. Our past is there to remind us, not define us. Allow your past experiences to push you toward relying on fresh, new practices.

These are a few of the significant differences between first and second marriages you should consider. They don't mean you're doomed. Unless you both refuse to address them that is.

1. **Navigating Child Relationships:** This is a tough one. Kids and cash are the one and two knockout punches for married couples. Parents battle over their own kids, so you know it's going to be intense within a blended family environment. While there is a sense of parental proprietorship for biological kids from a first marriage, stepparents may have an "on loan" attitude about their spouse's children. Child visitation schedules and an ever-present ex-spouse creates the sense of temporary toward the kids.

Additionally, adults don't hold the power cards over the kids' emotions and loyalties. Just because you love someone new doesn't mean they have to, or ever will. Similar to the 2005 classic movie, *Yours, Mine and Ours*, children no matter their ages, have an innate influence regarding influence equity.

First marriage parenting usually defines the role of each adult to include the care-taking, disciplinarian and mentor. Second marriages often stumble over any one of these items. Because discipline is the most dominant cause of failures, we examined the current schools of thought. And might I add that by the time we'd completed our meta-analysis, it was quite disturbing.

The academic recommendation suggests that a stepparent's role in disciplining their spouse's child should be similar to that of a nanny or babysitter whose job it is to observe and report bad behavior to the biological parent. The biological parent will then make the determination and degree of discipline and carry it out against their own child.

Can I confide that I almost gagged at these suggestions? This ideology rejects the bible-based marriage model of God as the head, then the parents and children next. Why would an adult who is already entering into a challenged environment relinquish their authority over a child?

I can just imagine Leah passively scribbling notes while Max breaks the house rules, and then waits for me to return home to punish him. But, had we not discussed our strategy with each other first and then with the kids, it would be as disastrous as the ineffective threats of, "Just wait until your father gets home."

It's also important to cover the stepparent's position as it relates to the kid(s). You must be sensitive to the fact that the child has also suffered great loss by their parents' divorce. While the adults can join CrossFit gyms and move forward with a newly contrived persona, the kids are ensnared in a vicious cycle of shared custody and limited visitations.

The new love in their parent's life must take time to establish an emotional connection with their spouse's children. It's a tough balance between being their friend and fulfilling the role of the third parent.

This is if divorce was the result, but what if their parent was remarrying after the death of their first spouse? This would become a very difficult scenario for taking the time to heal, recover and open their heart to another parent. So, go slow and as long as they aren't breaking the rules, give the kid a break so they get to know you, not the disciplinarian.

2. **Financial Baggage:** First marriages usually begin with no money but lots of hope for living on love. I know we all laughed at that, but seriously, there were no child support or alimony payments. Starting fresh but naïve was a blessing.

What money the first married couple makes goes toward fulfilling their dreams. Maybe it's a new car, house, boat or paying off student loans. No matter the priorities for their money, it is a team goal and team effort. Other than the government, there's no one jabbing fingers into their wallet.

A high percentage of people marry within two years of their first divorce being finalized. Within this short time span, or even up to the adult age that a biological parent is no longer obligated to pay child support, court-ordered payments create stress and sometimes financial hardships for the remarried parent and his new wife.

Additionally, those financial obligations create tension points and sometimes feelings of jealousy and resentment for the new spouse. The new spouse who works hard to contribute to their new family's household income is naturally resistant to paying a significant portion to their spouse's ex-spouse. The reverse may be true where the non-biological parent is resistant to factor their new spouse's support payments into the family budget. Each payment is a reminder that you were not your spouse's first choice.

Even in cases where there are no kids involved, the payment of alimony often causes more hardship than child support. At least with child support there is solace in hoping money goes toward benefitting the child. But, new spouses don't usually accept direct payments to an ex-spouse with much joy. While not always expressed, there is a high potential for resentment over those payments.

Child support and alimony are just two of the most obvious

examples. But either or both adults as is the normal course of life, rack up expenses and debt. Maybe it's being upside down on a car note, college student loans, credit cards or your half of the mortgage on the house you and your ex-spouse bought.

Debt is debt, and far too many adults rush into a second marriage without examining or disclosing finances. Even if it requires exchanges credit reports, take the time to understand your new love's level of security, indebtedness, legal payment obligations, bankruptcies and spending habits.

The last thing you want is to apply for a mortgage on a new dream home and find out your new spouse's credit score is even lower than the hundred bucks in their savings account. Money is a marriage killer. Get informed the second time around.

3. **Reconstructing Family Culture:** First married couples experience more challenges with which family of in-laws to visit for the holidays. Soon, they begin establishing their own traditions and holiday customs once kids enter the mix. And, if the is conflict over holiday activities, most couples will work to iron out the details by focusing on what's best for the kids.

These new family traditions are fun because they were created from a combination of scratch and a mixture of how both adults enjoyed their own families' holiday customs while growing up.

First families also set the original tone for what family is. Do they attend church together, hang out with friends, vacation with family, exercise, pick sides of the bed or even choose what type of dog they'll welcome into their original family.

The culture of first married families is usually a combination of the influences from each adult's extended family, personal expectations, peer pressures, and necessity. Regardless of which external factor creates the deepest meaning by defining culture for the couple, it becomes uniquely theirs.

Remarried couples seldom dig beyond their last marriage's customs and traditions for constructing ways to cope with holidays, vacations and in-laws visits. They either adapt one or the other spouse's tradition or avoid the event altogether.

When one spouse is pressured into observing a custom such as Christmas because it was the way the spouse had always done it for the sake of the child, then the non-biological parent is forced to play the surrogate role of the biological parent's ex-spouse for the sake of preserving tradition for the child.

Second marriages should deconstruct the old habits, and explore practices from their own and their spouse's family that began long before each adult's' first marriage. Both adults should work to create something that resembles as little as possible the traditions started by them and their ex.

Include the children in creating new traditions, and their very own customs will prevent competition and disappointment between the blended kids and reduce stress for each parent. Unless there are traditions steeped in religious significance, then family traditions are an opportunity for compromise and blended unity.

4. **Faith:** This isn't the topic most fought over, but not because everyone is in agreement. Religion, as in faithful belief, not as in the practice of doing church, is usually a by-product of the first couple. Either an agreement was reached before they married, religion isn't a priority so differences don't matter, or they came to know Christ as a couple in the same faith and religion.

For the first couple who divorces, it's not uncommon that the woman feels unwelcome and unsupported at the church she and her ex-spouse attended. Even if the couple were embedded with the community of the church, women are usually the ones given cold shoulders, from the pastoral staff to the congregation. Regardless of who caused the divorce, she gets the hint and never returns to that church.

Second marriages are more prone to conflicts in the practice of faith and denominations of church attendance. This usually stems from the practices held over from the first marriage. There's a unique dynamic that if both adults are active in their faith, they are more willing to compromise without shelving their practices.

In the cases where faith is not discussed prior to remarriage, it becomes a conflict and either divorce results or the faith practicing spouse attends church alone. Unfortunately, too many couples end up reducing or eliminating regular attendance.

5. Forced Sharing: What's mine is yours and yours is mine is expected in a marriage. But for second marriages, what's ours is also your ex-spouse's and my ex-spouse's and your kids get more while my kids get less, but ultimately, I don't get nearly what I should because we're forced to take care of everyone else first.

That no longer sounds romantic, does it? Feelings of helplessness often lead to emotions of hopelessness. Second spouses ensnared in legal obligations imposed on their new spouse etch away at the expectation of a redo. Stains from each adult's past make a clean start impossible.

Even if your new spouse remarried as a result of death, there are still forced shares between the two adults and the kids. History cannot be erased, nor can memories and experiences. This is something first couples do not have to carry around.

Sure, first timers should address the life each shared before that first wedding, but other than temporary relationships, school and odd life events, the new first spouse isn't forced to surrender their sovereignty to their first love's first love.

Other than emotional forced shares there are a slew of other situations where being the first and only is outside of the new spouse's control. What home are both adults living in? Was it either one's first home with their ex-spouse?

How about the sporty sports car you walked out of the divorce with? Clothes, appliances, food in the pantry, or even a pet, it doesn't really matter what it is, the fact is, second marriages do not have the joy or honor of being completely the first.

This is where both adults must seek opportunities to invest in time or materials that belong solely to them. Whether it's a plant or a new home, second marriages need anchors and reassurances that there are no ties or obligations to either ex-spouse.

Dear friend, this is the time to let go of those things you've held on to from the past, and focus on what makes your love feel welcome and comfortable. Communication and sensitivity are going to go a long way at this point.

17

DIVORCE PROOFING MARRIAGE

Have you ever made a store purchase and just as you check out, the salesman slips in the up-sales question: "Would you like to protect your new product with our guaranteed insurance plan?"

While we recommend against the extra insurance for a Pez dispenser, we definitely do suggest you take out marriage insurance. Where do you find the policy terms and conditions? They're laid out in black and white in the Bible. God's word is about relationships. The first is His love for you, and the rest is your love for each other.

> *"The Lord appeared to him from far away. 'I have loved you with an everlasting love; therefore I have continued my faithfulness to you.'"*
> *Jeremiah 31:3*

What worries us is that second divorces come much easier than the first. There is a lack of fear and sting of the unknown that's in the first one. It's like walking through a haunted house for the second time. Becoming desensitized at losing or failure is a callusing condition of the first tough rub. And while it may afford a bit of protection from the raw hurt, the willingness to open the door to a next divorce isn't a positive effect.

It's vital to enmesh your marriage in God's word. Some people wait for external accolades, usually on social media, about what a beautiful couple. Please don't fall for this again. Ground your value and marital security in God's word, not some stranger's Facebook post.

A quick note about prioritizing your marriage, is that culture has adulterated the pre-wedding rituals. Where there used to be a bridal shower for the blushing bride-to-be, there are now extravagant parties, trips and adventures that make everyone else blush. The wedding ceremony is not the marriage celebration. Too many adults rush to the wedding as their finish line and are left lost and empty when the realities of marriage begin.

Your bible-based marriage should be celebrated daily through consistent church attendance as a family, praying together as a couple, and each working diligently to make sure God remains at the center of your marriage.

Gender Roles

Gender roles are an area where there is no compromise. Have you and your spouse discussed the definitions and expectations for both submitting to God? It works, because of the hierarchy established by God. The wife submitting to her husband as the head of their household, and the husband giving of himself for the family as Christ gave for His bride, is the order God ordained. When we rebel and either refuse to function in this "chain of command," then the spiritual center of marriage is replaced by a self-centering. It's also true when spouses refuse to uphold their ordained responsibilities.

By divorce-proofing your marriage, both adults must accept that they were each independent, active people who now show willingness to surrender and compromise to one another. Mother's who have been forced to perform in the role of mom *and* dad will find that returning to only the role of mother isn't as easy as they may have thought.

Conversely, dads who have been used to the role of part-time thanks to custodial agreements, must now become a full-time parent for his and her kids. This is also an adjustment because of the loss of freedom to pursue interests outside of the family. Neither adult can just assume it'll work out. Praying God gives each the guidance to work toward fulfilling these roles is the first step in securing your heavenly insurance policy against divorce.

What is your expectation for the reality of waking up next to your new spouse? Is it all hearts, flowers and romance or have you made space for concessions, confessions, sacrifices, and shifts that must be made to accommodate one another? No matter how well you know each other, once married, unexpected differences, changes, and conflicts occur.

Praying Together

If you want to know what the one thing you can do as a couple to reduce the risk of divorce is, it is pray together every day. There is nothing that should trump your prayer time. We beg you. If you are about to get married, or have already tied the second or third knot, commit to pray with your spouse daily.

Leah and I discussed this early on in our relationship. We identified it as a priority for tethering to a God-centered marriage model, and often encouraged other couples to do the same. There was one problem in the beginning. I couldn't bring myself to initiate prayer. Leah wasn't led by God to start it because she'd been convicted it was my role as head of the house and spiritual leader. She was right.

After months of trying, I just could not force myself to open my mouth to pray with her. On my own, I was a chatterbox, but when it came time for us, nothing could force me to start. The longer I struggled, the more I worried why I couldn't do it. I knew Leah was worried too, but I'd avoid it when asked.

I kept praying to be able to pray, and the morning of my dad's funeral I collapsed across Leah's stomach. Physically and emotionally spent, I whispered, "I don't want to go."

It was then in the moment of complete emptiness that I understood I wasn't speaking to Leah. It was the beginning of pouring my heart out to God. It was an emotional awakening after feeling so depressed and worried about not praying, that God filled me with a renewed sense of peace about the funeral and about it being okay to pray with my wife.

Why is it so hard? For men, it is actually more difficult than imagined. Most men simply don't know how to get started. If it were a sport or fixing the car, we'd roll up our sleeves and get it done. When it comes to leading our wife in prayer, the proverbial brakes get mashed.

There's an intimidation factor for intimately praying with our spouse. What if our prayers are not significant or spoken eloquently enough? How about if we don"t say the right things or don"t know exactly what to say? Is my spouse going to lose respect for me?

Men, this is not a case of silence is golden. It"s a time for you to ask God for guidance and the words to speak. Praying should make us feel vulnerable. It"s God we're talking to after all.

Where to find the encouragement:

- Don"t try being courageous.
- Accept that you aren"t in charge
- Expect a blessing for your obedience
- Know you are not being judged by your spouse

Men, this isn"t a case of letting sleeping dogs lie. Get in the fight. Armor up with the word of God and allow Him to defeat your enemy.

He will bless your marriage for your faithfulness as spiritual leaders in your family.

How to start:

- Keep your prayers casual
- Schedule a set time each day
- Keep your prayers short but to the point
- Don't worry about memorizing scripture
- Open your mouth and your heart will follow
- Ask your spouse if there are prayer requests
- Be sensitive to the Holy Spirit's presence

Above the Radar

Once a couple goes all out in God''s service, it''s not uncommon for satan to begin mingling in their affairs. Praying couples mean they''re drawing ever closer to Christ. That closeness begins to squeeze out space for temptation and marital strife.

Christians have admitted to living below the spiritual radar in hopes of avoiding satan''s attentions. If you're avoiding God for the sake of avoiding conflict, then you already have satan's full attention.

An uncertain spouse with unconfessed sin may fear unintentional discovery by their spouse or may feel their Achilles heel will become a focal point that brings destruction to the marriage if old habits resurface.

I now understand why back then I was unable to pray with Leah. I had sin that had not been confessed. God knew my heart and He knew it was in no condition to pray as the leader in our family. It wouldn't take long until that prayer life opened up and revealed chambers of darkness and injury where confession and healing had to occur. Praying together saved and now prospers our marriage. A praying married couple is greatly cherished by God. Marriage is His creation and He will protect it if only you allow Him to come in.

18

SOUL MATES AND UNICORNS

They Do Not Exist

I didn't have to break the news to Leah. She already knew. And guess what, she wasn't upset. Maybe because I also understand I'm not her soul mate either. Now, before you go feeling sorry for either one of us —don't. The term soul mate has become distorted.

Maybe too often and in some weird way has morphed into a definition of emotion superseding that of love. Like this a ridiculous claim: "This person is my spouse, but that person is my soul mate." I'm sure you can figure out that those words are often used by a spouse to justify an affair, or a lingering affinity for a past crush.

Time Travelers

Soul mates don't exist in a bible-based marriage. God is the center, and alone provides for both spouses. The current soul mate ideal revolves around one person being all that the other person needs to complete them. This is an affront to Christ. God is crystal clear that He is enough.

I read an article from a very popular publication that listed ten elements of a soul mate. I was floored by the candy-coated bullet points used to determine whether you're connected to your soul mate, or "merely just in love." The article talked about "flashbacks," and claimed that the two souls would experience them as glimpses of their past life connections. Reincarnation is not a part of God's creation of marriage.

Love is not an emotion or a first sighting; That's attraction. Love requires choice, commitment and effort. Its rewards are God-approved, and have nothing to do with reincarnated spirits reconnecting as time goes by.

Opposites Attract

Another misconception wrapped up in the soul mate fallacy is perfect compatibility. Oftentimes opposites do attract. When God created woman for man, she was called helper. This is sometimes mistaken as man's sidekick like Robin is to Batman. This couldn't be further from God's truth.

I've mentioned this before, but want to continue focusing on it because it's vital to understanding the relationship God wants us to share with our spouse. The "helper" God created is *ezer* in the original Hebrew. It literally means vitally important and powerful acts of rescue and support. Not to complete, but to help. It's also the very same term used by God to describe the Holy Spirit.

You Complete Me

Each spouse is created to lean into God to provide for them and make them whole. Crediting another human being with a heavenly task such as completing them says God failed in His creation of that person, and thus requires an imperfect human to finish what God couldn't.

Genesis states that God created man in His own image. God is perfect, therefore God's image is perfect. And complete.

"Then God said, 'Let Us make man in Our image, according to Our likeness;
and let them rule over the fish of the sea and over the birds of the sky and
over the cattle and over all the earth, and over every creeping thing that
creeps on the earth.' God created man in His own image, in the image of
God He created him; male and female He created them."
Genesis 1:26-27

God is very clear that we are not to place anything or anyone above Him. Claiming another person is what it takes to make you whole, is to say you don't need God—you only need your soul mate. When you consider the impossible weight of responsibility you've placed on "Johnny" or "Sarah" to complete you, it's an unheavenly task to attempt or expect them to succeed.

The truth is, I love Leah. She is a Godly woman and I've learned so much from her as well as her allowing me to become the humble servant leader of our family. But, no matter how wonderful she is, my wife will never, ever be God. It's not realistic, nor would it be fair to expect her to be.

God's commandments warn against having other gods before Him. These gods can be your work, alcohol, exercise, money, your children or this person you're all ga-ga about. Anything that relegates God to second or third place has become a god that you've placed before him. He wants to provide for you so you may learn more about who He is.

"Thou shalt have no other gods before me. Thou shalt not make unto thee
any graven image, or any likeness of any thing that is in heaven above, or
that is in the earth beneath, or that is in the water under the earth. Thou
shalt not bow down thyself to them, nor serve them: for I the Lord thy God
am a jealous God, visiting the iniquity of the fathers upon the children unto
the third and fourth generation of them that hate me."

Exodus 20:3-5

"You shall have no other gods before me. You shall not make for yourself an image in the form of anything in heaven above or on the earth beneath or in the waters below. You shall not bow down to them or worship them; for I, the Lord your God, am a jealous God, punishing the children for the sin of the parents to the third and fourth generation of those who hate me, [10] but showing love to a thousand generations of those who love me and keep my commandments."
Deuteronomy 5:7-8

Made to Win

There are soul mates, but they aren't meandering spirits who reconnect through reincarnation along the arc of history. In a Christ-focused marriage, the uniting of two into one is the Godly mating of souls.

"For this reason a man shall leave his father and his mother, and be joined to his wife; and they shall become one flesh."
Genesis 2:24

There's no wonder why over 50% of all first marriages fail. Many relationships are based on the earthly soul mate misconception that it's universally designed or mystically meant to be. As that article I read earlier implied, *"The beauty of free will is that you can remain in or change any relationship as you see fit."*

How's that for zero commitment? I guess the article's secular meaning of soul mate involves the temporary satisfaction of attraction or lust. The loving people's negative connotation didn't go unnoticed, *"...two loving people who have settled for each other's strengths and weaknesses..."*

This article, which was written by some junior, assistant contributing editor at this magazine that only prints content for exposure and not pay, went viral. Yet, persuading couples to read the ultimate marriage guide created by God almighty continues to be a struggle.

If you want 100% assurance of matrimonial success, then follow God's desire for your marriage. He created it, He cherishes it, and He has never designed anything to fail—especially marriage.

> *"And over all these virtues put on love, which binds them all together in perfect unity."*
> *Colossians 3:14*

Leah knows she is my heavenly soul mate, because through Christ and marriage we've become one. One body, one mind, and one soul. As far as the sugary-sweet fantasy of finding the one soul you've known since the beginning of time, and the act of sharing flashbacks of earlier centuries when the two of you were together, it's ridiculous and Godless.

I can't even recall what I had for breakfast, much less if I knew Leah during the Mesozoic Era. Although, I'm sure she would've been just as gorgeous riding a dinosaur as she is driving her car. Of course, I know there were no humans during that period, but as long as we're talking fantasy soul mating, why not have a little fun?

How About More Fun

I wanted to have a little fun with that section above, but the truth is, for all of the effort it requires to secure your marriage from the secular and demonic temptations, there is no joy like that of becoming one of one in a God-centered marriage. And, speaking of fun, I have nothing on the topic of unicorns. It just looked catchy in the heading.

Whether it's your first or your second, or your "fill in the blank" marriage, God allows grace in areas we do not deserve. Love is a gift

God would never deny. Loving one another is also a gift God adores because it's why He created us in the first place. There's no secret to this. God created us to enjoy life with each other. God is life, and He wants to share true life with you.

To share life, it requires a marriage model. Because God uses the same model to share with us, He created marriage to share between you and your spouse. This is the key to the whole thing. God must be centered in your marriage, and not in a statue on the mantel. Keeping Him in your head, your heart and your holy prayers will guarantee a deeper, more intimate love relationship.

19

FINAL TAKEAWAY

God was crystal clear on moving us to write this book. Initially we hesitated while praying to make sure we'd both received His word. Leah and I have a tendency to launch full speed ahead at even the slightest hint of God's direction. We've found ourselves out in midfield looking back for God, only to discover He wasn't ready for us to round the bases yet.

The beauty of centering your marriage on God is that He will always be there, even when you find yourselves far off base. From the first words on the page to these last words I'm typing has taken over three years. To put that into perspective, Leah and I are both accomplished authors. I can write a full-length novel in less than three weeks. Leah has actually written a book in about a week and a half (but it wasn't fun for anyone living within ten miles of our home).

Writing any book involves the editing process. You usually present your best efforts to someone who is skilled at reading through what you've created. They suggest changes and deletions, along with many corrections. It's all so you become a better writer, and you present a better message to the reader. You've really got to put your ego aside while the editor is digging into what you felt was your best effort. It can get super uncomfortable and sometimes painful to watch your best work get shredded before it can become something of value to others.

What neither of us knew when we began this book years ago was that the editor was going to be God, and we were the pages that got worked over. We started out writing like a rocket. We thought we'd finish in a month and start on the next book. It was all so easy. But as we tend to do, we became secure and confident—almost cocky. After all, it was a book about life after divorce and the remarriage process. We'd been there and done that.

What we didn't realize was that while we physically moved through the processes to understand the practical applications, we'd missed the deeper spiritual implications. We were skilled at putting our words on paper, but we hadn't waited to seek what words God wanted written. We were sharing the academic realities of life after divorce, while God wanted an opening of our hearts to share our lives, not just our learning.

We've been honest with you the entire way, so it won't stop now. We set this book aside about half way through as our marriage ran viciously ashore. The year we thought would be spent spinning out books on remarriage and blending families turned into the roughest year either of us had ever experienced. There were days, weeks, and months worrying about not how we'd hang on, but *if* we'd hang on.

I will tell you that never once did we ever consider divorce. Why not? Because it was the curse of our pasts. We were not going to allow satan to beat us into fleeing to the days of turning away from the person God wanted us to turn to. Everything we've written in this book, we practice. From death to debt to deceit to doubt, the years of "editing" were at times more than we thought we could handle. And to be honest, it was much more than we could handle on our own. But with Christ as the core, we weathered the storms.

We picked up the book writing project about a year after first logging out of the word processing program. We cried as we read through the first few chapters. The two people who wrote those first words no longer existed. We knew the force of God's power and the depth of His love as we combed over the first half of this book. We knew it had to be rewritten from the very beginning. It was no longer an instruction manual, but God's love story of our testimony.

This is us witnessing to you about the truth of God's promise and hope He has for your life. He holds you dear to His heart. Your divorce crushed Him as much as it hurt you. God is the real deal, and if you are serious about recovering from divorce and even starting over in a new relationship, He is the only way.

We're so thankful to have been blessed to share this resource for loving life after divorce with you. Leah and I were praying together toward the end of this project and I was praising Him for the work He invested in us so we could create the right message to share. I said something about the next book, and God was again crystal clear in His word.

God said, "Writing the book about writing this book will be your next book."

I held Leah even tighter because His words were so convicting. I knew the story of what He'd done for us while we were writing to help you was actually as much about helping us. We cannot wait share that next story with you.

You were meant for so much more. Claim that victory for your life today!

Scott & Leah

This book took more years than we'd planned on to write, and there were a lot of people who helped us along the way. Thank you to Josh Melancon, Matt Sessoms, and Chermaine Stein for getting us on track. We owe you more than we could ever repay, and we love you all.

Thank you to Dar Albert at Wicked Smart Designs and Kim Cannon for all your work on making this book a reality.

ABOUT THE AUTHORS

Dr. Scott and Leah Silverii have both survived the soul-shattering trauma of divorce. They also know the beauty of restoration. Walk with them through the process and into the light of recovery.

Dr. Scott Silverii and his wife Leah have blended seven kids and a French Bulldog named Bacon into a wonderfully unique family. Their passion is helping the hurting. They are the founders of Blue Marriage, a ministry that mentors law enforcement marriages. They also serve on the staff at *MarriageToday*.

Scott, a retired chief of police, holds a PhD from the University of New Orleans and is working towards his Doctor of Ministry from The

King's University. Leah is a *New York Times* and *USA Today* bestselling author of over sixty works of fiction.

When not spending time with family, they enjoy crossing the country on their motorcycle, and hanging out with friends in their hometown of Dallas, Texas.

Lets Connect:
Website Contact

NOTES

2. Denial and Isolation:

1. Daveduik Gingrich, Heather (2013) Restoring the Shattered Self: A Christian Counselor's Guide to Complex Trauma, InterVarsity Press.
2. Chapman, Gary (2014) One More Try What to Do When Your Marriage Is Falling Apart. Moody Publishers.
3. Evans, Tony (2012) Divorce and Remarriage. Moody Publishers
4. Mason, Karen (2014) Preventing Suicide: A Handbook for Pastors, Chaplains and Pastoral Counselors. IVP Books.

3. Anger

1. Smalley, Gary (2015) From Anger to Intimacy How Forgiveness Can Transform Your Marriage. Revell
2. Sande, Ken (2004). The Peacemaker: A Biblical Guide to Resolving Personal Conflict. Baker Books.

4. Bargaining

1. Turner, Victor (1970) The Forest of Symbols: Aspects of Ndembu Ritual. Cornell Press

8. Spiritual Grounding

1. Batterson, Mark (2016) The Circle Maker: Praying Circles Around Your Biggest Dreams and Greatest Fears. HarperCollins Publishing

14. Before You Say "I Do"

1. FamilyLife Weekend To Remember (2017) FamilyLife Ministries.

CPSIA information can be obtained
at www.ICGtesting.com
Printed in the USA
LVHW011607160120
643871LV00006B/1103